Quality Circles

Quality Circles

How to Make Them Work in America

Philip C. Thompson

amacom

AMERICAN MANAGEMENT ASSOCIATIONS

Library of Congress Cataloging in Publication Data

Thompson, Philip C.
  Quality circles.

  Includes index.
  1. Quality circles—United States. I. Title.
HD66.T48   658.4'036   82-4072
ISBN 0-8144-5731-2   AACR2

First Printing

Preface

I address this book first to managers who are interested in putting quality circles into effect in their organizations, and second to program administrators, trainers, and advisors who are charged with installing quality circles. My aim is to provide them with a clear understanding of the quality circle concept and process, the goal of a quality circle installation program, the steps they must take to achieve this goal, the benefits they will reap for the organization if they follow these steps, and the problems they will encounter if they do not.

The need for such a book increases daily. A few years ago, the number of organizations in the United States with quality circles numbered less than a dozen. Today there are hundreds, if not thousands. This rapid growth has occurred without benefit of experience. We have learned the basics of quality circles. We know how they should work in the abstract and what they achieve when they are successful. All of that can be gotten easily in the available literature, but we do not yet know how to install them successfully.

In this book I try to codify the lessons of three years of experience in designing and implementing a quality circle installation program. In carrying out this task, I have chosen to emphasize the practical aspects of quality circles and to avoid theory. To this end, I first describe the quality circle process and the characteristics of an organization with fully developed quality circles. Then, I present the material on installation in a "how to" fashion, beginning with the first step and proceeding to the last. At each step I have included discussions of the logical options and their consequences, good and bad. I have illustrated my points with numerous case histories.

I have chosen also to present problems, pitfalls, and outright failures. I do this in the belief that gaining experience is a matter of learning to recognize and avoid danger, as well as knowing when to seize opportunities. Too many books tell us *how* to without telling us how *not* to.

It is difficult to install quality circles. It takes planning, patience, commitment, and, above all, a clear understanding of what you are doing and why. Unfortunately, many people try to sell quality circles as a quick and easy fix—the going fad. Managers, in turn, too readily accept the idea without understanding what they are getting into or even why they are doing it. When the inevitable problems arise, they are unprepared and take the easy way out. They terminate the program, convinced that the concept will not work. In truth, they never gave it a chance. This is a shame, because most of our organizations desperately need quality circles, or institutions like them, if they are to survive in an increasingly competitive world.

• • •

The Japanese invented quality circles as the final link in their drive to apply the techniques of statistical quality control. In fact, their English term for the concept is quality *control* circle. But once developed, Japanese quality control circles quickly became more than instruments for involving workers in the process of controlling product quality. Their functions broadened. Workers presented proposals on improving productivity, increasing shop safety, and, in some cases, enhancing product design. Management listened and accepted their ideas. The quality control circle very quickly became a vehicle for limited worker participation in management decisions.

In this sense, the terms "quality control circle" and

"quality circle" are both misleading. "Worker participation groups," or something similar, would be more descriptive. However, in the United States the term quality circle has acquired wide currency, and I will not try to buck that historical precedent.

Because the Japanese invented the quality circle and have spent twenty years perfecting its use, it would seem logical to copy their system. Not so. We should analyze their system and borrow what appears useful, as they borrowed from us, but we should be wary of wholesale transplants.

In Japan, quality circles exist in an environment of worker identity with the organization, commitment to consensus decision making by groups, and a great deal of concern over employee welfare. By contrast, in the United States, workers identify with their skill, trade, or profession. They are welders first, employees of the organization second. Decision-making styles, while widely divergent, tend to be adversarial and individualistic in nature. People confront each other with positions. They compete. Someone wins, others lose. Most organizations do not concern themselves with employee welfare. That job is left to the public sector.

In my view, we *need* quality circles, but we have to learn how to adapt them to our organizational environment. We can get a lot of good hints from the Japanese, but, in the end, we are going to have to find our own way to make the generalized quality circle concept work for us.

My understanding of quality circles and the quality circle process derives from personal experience at Martin Marietta Corporation, Michoud Division of Denver Aerospace in New Orleans and from conversations with other program administrators and advisors around the country. Accordingly, I have adapted the thirty-one case studies presented throughout the text directly from firsthand experiences at Michoud or secondhand incidents recounted to me by others. I have changed contexts, circumstances, and names to protect the privacy of individuals involved, but otherwise they are factual.

• • •

I wish to thank the employees of Martin Marietta Corporation, Michoud Division, for it is they who taught and continue to teach me what will and will not work in a quality circle effort. I also wish to thank that company, and expecially Ken Timmons, vice president and general manager of Michoud Division, for his intuitive understanding of the worth of quality circles and his unfailing support of our efforts. I owe special thanks to my colleagues Ralph Tortorich, Bob Lozano, Constantine Orfan, Christine Dreyfus, Michael Kelley, Denise Layfield, Russell Arthur, Charles Rock, Andrew Kaslow, Debbie Berkman, and Sandra Pace—all of whom have contributed directly and indirectly to this work.

I would like to acknowledge an indirect but significant debt to friends and colleagues of the board of directors and the officers of the International Association of Quality Circles: Bob Cole, Jeff Beardsley, Price Gibson, Wayne Rieker, Don Dewar, Fred Riley, Young Lee, Jill King, John Keefe, Jim Stansbury, Bob Amsden, Bill Courtwright, Sud Ingle, Howard Ferguson, Bonnie Hunt, Vern Pagano, Bob Pearce, Bob Scott, George Sederberg, George Youst, Elija Douglas, and Rick Stokes.

I owe special thanks to Judy Bules and Walt Herip for their personal support, to Margie Reyes for her excellent typing, and Annette Harper for her illustrations. Most of all, I am indebted to Jan Garrett. She encouraged me to undertake this book and willingly assumed the task of reading and commenting on the first draft. Without her support and help I probably would not have completed it.

Philip C. Thompson

Contents

Part One   Understanding Quality Circles

1   Quality Circles and the Quality Circle Process   *3*
2   The Japanese Success Story: Toyota Auto Body   *18*

Part Two   Installing Quality Circles

3   Installation: What Can Go Wrong   *31*
4   Institutionalizing the Quality Circle Office   *42*
5   Strategies and Implementation   *65*
6   Training   *100*
7   Preparing the Organization   *109*
8   Working Out the Details   *132*

Part Three   Interpreting the Quality Circle Process

9   A Political Process   *177*

Index   *190*

PART ONE
Understanding Quality Circles

1

Quality Circles and the Quality Circle Process

A quality circle is a small group of employees and their supervisor from the same work area, who voluntarily meet on a regular basis to study quality control and productivity improvement techniques, to apply these techniques to identify and solve work-related problems, to present their solutions to management for approval, and to monitor the implementation of these solutions to ensure that they work.

Some Specific Details

- Quality circles are small. They range in size from four to fifteen members. Eight is optimum.
- All members come from the same shop or work area. This shop or work area gives the circle its identity.
- The members work under the same supervisor, who is a member of the circle.
- The supervisor is usually, though not always, the

leader of the circle. As leader, he or she moderates discussion and promotes consensus. The supervisor does not issue orders or make decisions. The circle members, as a group, make their own decisions.

• Voluntary participation means that everyone in a shop or office has an opportunity to join, to refuse to join, to postpone joining, to quit, and to rejoin.

• Circles usually meet once every week on company time, with pay.

• Circles usually meet in special meeting rooms removed from their normal area.

• Circle members receive special training in the rules of quality circle participation, the mechanics of running a meeting and making management presentations, and the techniques of group problem solving such as brainstorming, cause-and-effect analysis, flow charts, and Pareto analysis.

• Circle members, not management, choose the problems and projects that they will work on.

• Circles collect all the information and help they can in analyzing a problem and developing a solution.

• Technical specialists and management in general assist circles with information and expertise whenever asked to do so.

• Circles receive advice and guidance from an advisor who attends all circle meetings but who is not a circle member.

• Management presentations are given to those managers and technical specialists who would normally make the decision on a proposal.

• Circles exist as long as the members wish to meet. They can declare themselves inactive; they can reactivate themselves at a later date; they may exist for only one or two months, or for years, solving hundreds of problems, or only one or two.

CASE #1
Drilling Holes

The Mechanical Assembly Quality Circle works the second shift, between 4:00 P.M. and midnight. Its members, five assemblers and their supervisor, spend most of their time drilling holes in aluminum and installing fasteners of various types. One member, Clive, a lifelong union man, is over sixty. Another, Dexter, is black, in his mid-forties. The rest—John, a Liberian national, Miguel, of Mexican origin, and Mike—are all under thirty. Marvin, the supervisor, is an ex-sergeant in his mid-thirties. He leads the meetings. Frank, their advisor, trained them in problem-solving techniques and attends most of their meetings, advising them on procedures and helping with viewgraphs and paperwork.

When they formed the circle, the members were unclear about which problem they would tackle first. They considered various things: a tool that broke down repeatedly, the chronic shortage of parts, poor drawings. Discussion over several meetings led them to conclude that they could solve none of the problems themselves. So, after some debate, they decided to turn to the problem of shanking fasteners.

Many of the holes they drilled were slightly crooked, causing the fasteners to skew when inserted. Each of these shanking fasteners had to be drilled out and a new, larger hole redrilled for a new fastener. The problem was an "unofficial" one. The quality inspector seldom wrote a discrepancy report on these fasteners, but the assemblers could recognize the error, knew it would fail inspection, and repaired it before calling the inspector. Still, it was time consuming and irritating to redo work.

As a first step toward solving the problem, the circle members systematically analyzed the areas in the assembly where they were encountering the largest number of shanking fasteners. Drawing on their experience, they identified eight areas, seven involving poor access to the drilling surface and one involving a long stretch of freehand drilling. Having isolated these causes of the problem, they decided that the best solution was to design a tool or aid for each area that would keep the drill bit straight.

In the next few meetings the members drew alternative designs on the blackboard and discussed their merits. Unfortunately, none of them seemed adequate. After eight sessions it looked as though the solution might prove as difficult as the problem. Then, one evening, when the session was about to begin, Dexter entered the meeting room with a grin on his face. He sat down with the other members and announced that Mike had something to say. Mike had never spoken during the previous meetings. Coaxed and badgered by Dexter, he finally revealed his secret. He had an idea for one tool that they could use in all eight areas. As he drew it on the board, it was clear that here was the best solution—a simple tool that would allow them to drill virtually all holes error-free. As an added benefit, it would cut down set-up time to an insignificant fraction of what it had been. The circle members were elated.

During the following week, Marvin, the supervisor, took the rough drawing to the night-shift engineer who made a more professional drawing. Then, for the next four sessions the members prepared viewgraphs and rehearsed their lines, guided by their advisor who acted as a kind of stage director. Once they felt that they were ready, they set a time and a place for their management presentation and invited all the people whose input was necessary for a decision to implement their proposal.

When the time came, the invited managers filed into the conference room, grumbling at having to stay late. The circle members were understandably nervous. There they stood before their bosses, and even their bosses' bosses, telling *them* how to solve a problem. But their rehearsals paid off. They sounded logical and articulate. Each member presented a section—introduction of the circle members and statement of the problem, analysis and determination of causes, history of previous attempts at a solution, their solution, and a cost-benefit analysis to strengthen their case.

The managers received the pitch a bit skeptically. Most were hard-bitten middle management types, conditioned to giving direct orders to the very employees standing before them and very unaccustomed to hearing these employees voice opinions, much less logical analyses of complex problems. Nevertheless, they admitted the worth of the proposal, investigated its compatibility with engineering and tooling, and, two weeks later, concluded that the tool was feasible and would be a tremendous improvement to the production process. They ordered it built.

Once management decided to implement the proposal, the circle leader and advisor filled out a project status report, listing the attending managers as well as the actions they agreed to see carried out. This sheet went directly to the planning office which, over the next three months, tracked the progress of the design and production of the tool. In the meantime, the circle members themselves kept watch on the progress of their tool through frequent telephone calls to the tool design department.

The cost savings for the project, as estimated by the circle and validated by management, were approximately $7,000 per production unit over the life of the project (approximately twenty years). With an estimated saving of $14,000 during the first year, a total cost for the tool of $500, and a cost of $2,880 for the time spent by the circle members in developing the idea (six men at $20 per hour for twenty-four hours), the savings-to-cost ratio was five to one.

The Mechanical Assembly Quality Circle continues to meet, but its membership has changed. Miguel and John now work in quality inspection rather than manufacturing. Marvin and Clive moved back to first shift where they joined another circle. Mike and Dexter are working with a new employee and a new supervisor on another project, the design of a workstand for a particularly difficult installation.

CASE #2
Paying Bills

Women make up the Accounts Payable Quality Circle. The leader is Ruth, supervisor of the other members. They include Wilhelmina, Venita, Mona, Germaine, Gwendolyn, Dottie, and Mary. They have been meeting for six months, every Friday afternoon. An advisor attends regularly to provide help and advice when needed.

Following their initial training in group problem-solving techniques, the circle listed a total of thirty-six problems that plagued their work. The most urgent of these dealt with delayed payment to vendors on direct charge accounts. These delays were getting worse, and some vendors had threatened to ship materials C.O.D. The good name of the organization was under fire, but more important, the group felt that it was *their* problem and that they alone could and would solve it.

They knew the immediate cause for the delay: invoices for direct charge accounts arrived in their office with incomplete or incorrect information and, as a result, they were unable to pay vendors until the complete and correct information was obtained. To make matters worse, no quick and easy way to obtain the information existed.

The circle decided to track the overall invoice error rate, the specific types of errors, and the origins of these errors. For two weeks they designed a detailed check sheet applicable to all invoice routes. Then, over the next three weeks, they tracked the invoices and discovered an astounding 50 percent error rate. Their check sheet also showed that the errors occurred both in-house and at the vendors.

The circle members chose to concentrate on reducing in-house errors first. This meant contacting everyone within the organization who dealt with direct charge accounts and acquainting them with the problem. In addition, they developed a sheet to attach to any invoice found to be in error. The sheet routed the invoice through an error-correction loop. As they proceeded with this approach, the rate of invoices with errors entering their office dropped to 35 percent.

Next, they decided to talk to the vendors. With the help of the purchasing department, they spoke informally to all the designated vendors, telling them to fill out invoices completely and correctly if they wished payment. They followed this with a written advisory which included specific, documented cases in which vendors had failed to fill out the invoices correctly. In addition, they called in all the vendors for a meeting, confronted them with the problem, and walked them through the requirements of the program and the invoices. When a vendor stated or implied that he did not make mistakes, the circle members politely presented him with more documented cases. This second stage in the solution occurred over three weeks. At the end of this period, the tracking showed a reduction in errors to approximately 17 percent.

Finally the circle returned to the in-house errors. The members decided that the only way to resolve the problem permanently was to revise the system. To do this, they first documented each of the invoice routes, noting the offices through which they passed and the signatures that appeared. Once they understood the existing routes, they began to analyze them with an eye to reducing the number of routes and signatures. Eventually, they produced a plan for a much more streamlined routing system, as well as a final version of their corrective action form and a list of individuals along the route to whom a request for corrections could be sent.

At this point, the circle members felt that they needed management approval to implement the new system fully. To obtain it, they prepared a management presentation describing the problem and its impact, the investigation, the solutions they had already implemented, and the proposal to modify the system. They proudly highlighted a control chart showing the progressive decrease in invoice errors from 50 percent to 17 percent, with the indication of a goal of 5 percent or less. Like the mechanical assemblers, each member took a speaking part, wrote her own statements, and made the viewgraphs to illustrate them. They set a date and invited the managers concerned, fifteen in all.

The presentation went well. Most of the managers were overwhelmed by the magnitude of the problem and delighted with the solution already in effect. With the exception of a few minor changes to accommodate certain audit requirements, management accepted the new plan and agreed to an implementation schedule. Within three weeks of the presentation, the Accounts Payable Quality Circle reduced the defective invoices to below 5 percent and has since held it there.

No actual cost savings were calculated for this project, but another division of the company was forced to drop its direct charge program and return to a more expensive purchase requisition procedure because it was unable to solve similar problems.

Organizational Results

Once installed, quality circles produce dramatic results for an organization. They improve morale, increase a sense of loyalty to the organization, and foster a sense of teamwork among employees who participate. They improve overall productivity of the organization, and they improve the quality of the product or service. And they reduce grievances, lost time, accidents, scrap, attrition, absenteeism, and tardiness. In short, they solve problems and save the organization money.

These claims are not exaggerated. Though data on results in the United States are limited, there are enough to show that quality circles live up to their press. The following are a few examples from published sources.

Honeywell: * 1. In a nonunion electronics assembly shop of high-technology, high-reliability, and low-volume work, 10 circles with 120 members reduced costs by 46 percent over a 2-year period.

2. In a nonunion hybrid microelectronics laboratory of high-volume and technologically complex work, 11 circles with 94 members solved 109 problems over a 9-month period. These amounted to $86,430 of documented savings, a 36 percent reduction in assembly costs per unit, and significant improvements in cooperation, management response, communication, feedback, participation, effec-

* Michael Donovan and Bill Van Horn, "Quality Circle Program Evaluation," *The Second Annual IAQC International Conference Transactions,* 1980, pp. 99–101. Available from the International Association of Quality Circles, P.O. Box 30635, Midwest City, Oklahoma 73140.

tiveness, and satisfaction, as measured by an in-house attitude questionnaire.

3. In a machine shop with heavy, out-of-date equipment involving complex work, half of 250 unionized employees formed circles. Half did not. Over a nine-month period, the employees in circles improved equipment use by 9 percent over employees not in circles.

Martin Marietta Corporation, Michoud Division: * 1. In a facility dedicated to mechanical and weld assemblies and to the application of various thermal protection materials, 142 circle members improved their rate of defects per person from .49 for the six months before joining to .20 for the six months after joining. During equivalent time periods, 409 nonmembers improved their rate from .40 to .30. Thus although the nonmembers began with a better rate, they improved it by only 25 percent, while the circle members improved their rate by 59 percent.

2. In the same facility, circle members improved their lost time record from 65.32 hours per person per six-month period for the last half of 1980 to 39 hours for the first half of 1981. Nonmembers, during the same time period, improved from 75.68 to 63.68. That is, the rate of improvement for members was 40 percent, while the rate for nonmembers was only 16 percent.

General Dynamics/Pomona Division: † 1. For the six months before joining a circle, only 13.7 percent of future circle members submitted suggestions. In the six months after joining, 74.7 percent of these people submitted

---

* R. Tortorich, P. Thompson, C. Orfan, D. Layfield, C. Dreyfus, and M. Kelley, "Measuring the Organizational Impact of Quality Circles," *The Quality Circles Journal*, November 1981. Available from the International Association of Quality Circles.

† Bonnie Hunt, "Measuring Results in a Quality Circles Pilot Test," *The Quality Circles Journal*, August 1981.

suggestions. During the same time periods, submissions dropped from 8.8 percent to 6.7 percent for all other employees.

2. Over the same year period, the attrition rate for quality circle members was 8 percent while the overall rate was 25 percent.

None of these numbers capture the sense of energy and excitement unleashed by quality circles among employees. Most workers, whether they move hardware or paper, have little or no opportunity to make a positive contribution to their work. They do their job, which is often boring and monotonous, but never have a chance to voice their ideas about doing it better, faster, or more safely. That they can make a contribution is obvious. After all, the same people doing monotonous, mindless work all day go home to families, whose housing, feeding, education, and finances they manage quite adequately. Given the opportunity, they can apply this same intelligence and energy to their work.

Once, after presenting the quality circle concept to a group of forklift drivers, I turned the meeting over to them for discussion on whether they wanted to form a circle. One side quickly decided in favor. The other side, the minority, argued that this kind of work was management's job, not theirs. They saw quality circles as just another management "scam." Yes, they knew ways to improve their job, but why should they? The argument continued, and it seemed that they would never reach a decision. Finally an older man, who had been listening patiently, commented that he had worked for many companies in which he was prohibited from speaking his mind and voicing his ideas about how to do the work. "Here is a chance to have a say, and I'm going to take it." All of them eventually joined the circle.

Structure and Process

The term "quality circle" has two meanings. It refers to both a structure and process and to a group of people and the activities they undertake. Thus, we can speak of a "quality circle process" as well as a "quality circle."

Structure: The structure of a quality circle is basically the composition of the group, defined by the positions of its members in the wider organization. Diagram 1 illustrates the structure of a typical quality circle within a hypothetical organization. It represents an ideal, a goal to strive for. In practice, quality circles require a long period of tutelage by an advisor. Therefore, Diagram 2 more accurately represents the structure of a quality circle.

Process: The quality circle process contains four sub-processes:

1. Identification of problems, intense study of quality and productivity improvement techniques, and development of solutions.

2. Review, in a management presentation, of the circle's proposed solution by involved managers and technical specialists to decide whether or not to implement it.

3. Implementation of the solution by the wider organization.

4. Evaluation of the success of the solution by the circle and the organization.

Diagram 3 illustrates this process.

How, then, do we go about installing the quality circle process in an organization? The rest of the book will attempt to answer this question, first by describing an organization with fully developed quality circles.

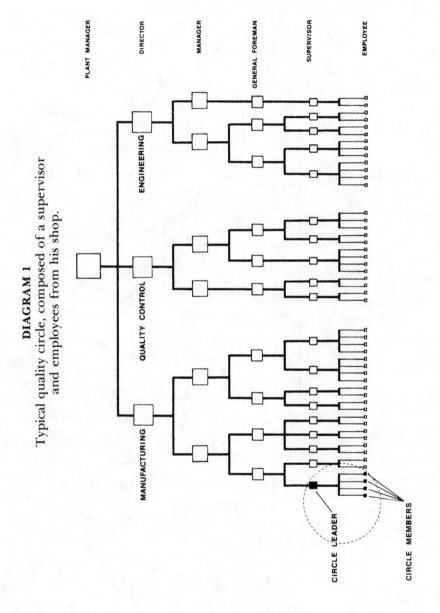

DIAGRAM 1

Typical quality circle, composed of a supervisor and employees from his shop.

DIAGRAM 2

Typical quality circle with an advisor assisting
the leader and members.

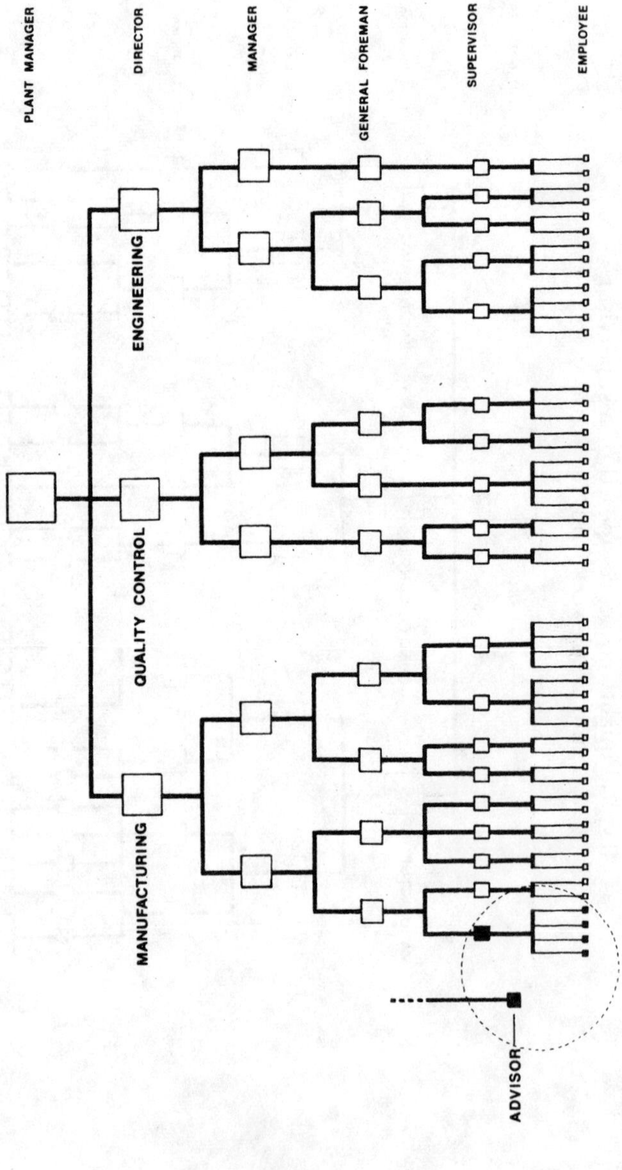

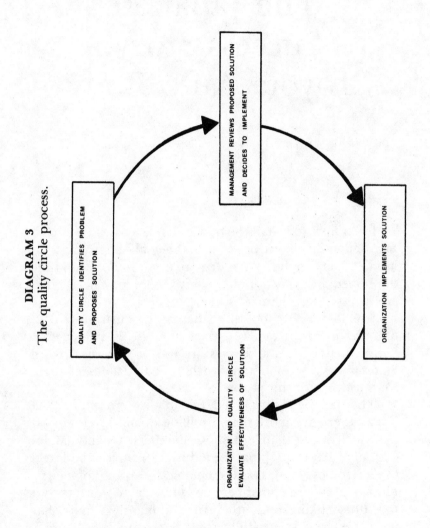

DIAGRAM 3
The quality circle process.

2
The Japanese Success Story: Toyota Auto Body

To learn how to install the quality circle process, we must first define the objective. What is the goal of a program to install quality circles? What does an organization with fully developed and functioning quality circles look like? What are its essential characteristics?

The logical way to answer these questions is to find an organization with quality circles and use it as a model. Unfortunately, quality circles are too new in the United States to have become standardized. To find a model, then, we must turn to the Japanese.

The Japanese developed the quality circle in 1962. Today there are more than a million quality circles in Japan, with more than 8 million members. Quality circles exist in nearly every Japanese industry, from iron and steel to electronics, food, textiles, chemicals, and automobiles. Most quality circle members are blue-collar workers, but recently banking and other predominantly white-collar industries have successfully applied the concept. There is every reason to expect the number of Japanese quality circles to continue to grow for many years to come.

This extensive distribution, covering a wide variety of situations and organizations, produces many variations in the way individual organizations promote and maintain quality circles. Most of these differences are superficial, however, and within all organizations there is a consistent and logical pattern. The best way to illustrate this pattern is to consider one such organization in detail.

Toyota Auto Body *

Toyota Auto Body produces bodies for passenger cars, trucks, and commercial vans, most of which it sells to Toyota Motor Company. There are two main plants, one in Kariya (commercial vans) and one in Fujimatsu (cars and trucks). Most of the work occurs on assembly lines and involves sheetmetal working, pressing, painting, assembling, and shipping. In 1979, Toyota Auto Body had 6,293 employees, three fourths of them blue-collar workers.

Number of circles: Toyota Auto Body began promoting quality circles in 1964, at the same time that circles were promoted throughout Toyota Motor Company. By 1968, there were 226 active circles in the company, and by 1971 there were 279. As of 1981, the number had expanded to 841 quality circles.

Participation rate: Participation in quality circles is voluntary. In 1974, approximately 4,000 employees, most of them blue-collar, participated in quality circles. Many people belonged to more than one. That figure represented 72 percent of all employees.

* Robert E. Cole, *Work, Mobility, and Participation: A Comparative Study of American and Japanese Industry,* Berkeley, Calif.: University of California Press, 1979, pp. 156–167; Union of Japanese Scientists and Engineers, "Outline of Toyota Auto Body Co., Ltd.," *Reports of QC Circle Activities,* No. 13, 1980, p. 74.

Number of projects: The number of projects produced by these circles has held steady. In 1973, there were 1,787 successful projects. In 1979, there were 1,791 successful projects. Using the 1979 figures, simple division shows that the average number of projects completed per circle per year was 2.13.

Leadership, pay, and meeting time: Originally, supervisors led quality circles at Toyota Auto Body, but by 1969, senior workers had replaced supervisors in many circles. Some leaders are even elected or serve on a rotation basis. Circles meet after regular hours and members receive overtime pay at half their regular pay. In the beginning, circles met only once a month, but by 1975 they were meeting as often as six times each month.

Technical assistance: To provide technical assistance to quality circles, Toyota Auto Body formed an Industrial Engineering Project team. It has forty-five members, half of whom are engineers and half of whom are shop employees who have received special training. The rationale behind this division of labor is that the mix of shop personnel and engineers provides more innovative contributions to solutions than engineers alone. The services of the team are available to all circles when needed.

Incentives: The company promotes two major kinds of incentives for participation in quality circles: competition and money. With respect to the former, circles compete regularly for the best solution to the problem and the best presentation at the department level. Each month, the best of these compete against those of other departments for companywide honors. Finally, the best in the company enter regional and national competitions sponsored by the Japanese Union of Scientists and Engineers.

With respect to financial incentives the company pays for quality circle participation. As previously noted, it pays half the regular wages for each hour of quality circle meeting time. In addition, it pays more for suggestions submitted by quality circles than it pays for suggestions from individuals. The best suggestions from individuals receive $227, whereas the best from circles receive $272. Interestingly, the company requires all sections to submit a certain number of suggestions each year and pays for them, even if they are not adopted ($2.27 to individuals and $2.72 to circles). On the average, 75 percent of all suggestions submitted come from quality circles.

Finally, but most important, the company pays as much as the equivalent of five months' wages to all its employees, even blue-collar workers, in the form of bonuses. The total amount of bonus funds available is determined by negotiations between the union and the company, and depends on the company's performance and the overall economic climate. Individual bonuses, however, are based on age, job, skill, and performance, with performance being the most important. Within the context of this pay system, voluntary participation in quality circles is an obvious way for a worker to demonstrate commitment and interest and to attain greater skill and knowledge about the job, thus improving performance and, in the end, increasing his or her bonus.

Promotion: To promote, train, and coordinate quality circle activities, the company has set up an elaborate system of offices and interlocking circles illustrated in Diagram 4. At the top is the quality circle general office, which reports to the plant manager. It holds responsibility for plantwide planning for all quality circle activities. In particular, it coordinates the selection of the best problem-solving project and the circle which will represent the company in the regional and national competitions. Below this office, in each department there is a quality circle department office responsible for planning and promoting the program in that department. It develops the necessary

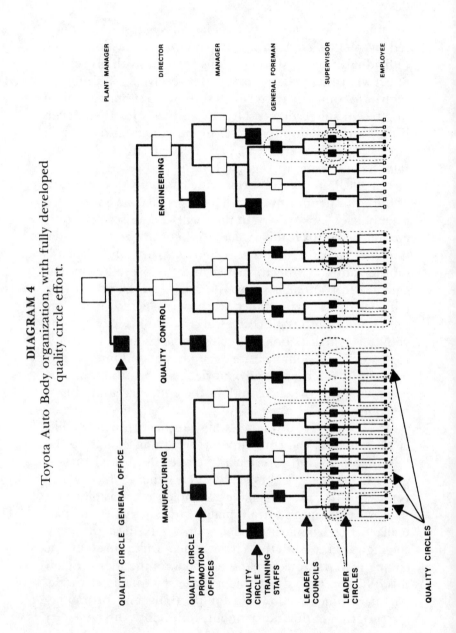

DIAGRAM 4

Toyota Auto Body organization, with fully developed quality circle effort.

training materials for circle members and circle leaders. At the section level, a special staff implements the training program developed at the department office. This group also runs monthly intrasectional meetings of quality circle leaders, in which information is exchanged, problem-solving topics are discussed, and mutual support is established. Finally, a leader council, or conference, including the general foreman, the supervisors, and the quality circle leaders who are not supervisors, coordinates circle activities with company policies and guides circles in the selection of problems.

Training: Training for circle members emphasizes study of actual problem-solving cases, as well as analytical and statistical techniques such as flow diagrams, charts, histograms, and Pareto analysis. Special training for circle leaders focuses on the proper way to conduct meetings and to encourage workers to speak up and participate.

Evaluating results: Officials of Toyota Auto Body report the following kinds of evidence to illustrate the success and benefits of quality circles:

- New techniques and machinery suggested by quality circles.
- Awards won by their quality circles in regional and national competitions.
- Decline in defect rates from .95 defects per car completed in 1968 to .60 defects per car completed in 1973.
- Reduction in man-hours per car from ten in 1968 to eight in 1973.
- Reduction in accidents from 53 per million man-hours worked to zero in 1972.
- Decline in employee turnover from 18.2 percent in 1968 to 8.5 percent in 1973.
- A rise in proportion of workers who feel their work is

worth doing, from 29 percent to 45 percent in 1973, shown by annual attitude surveys.

• Overall improvement in worker skills, with special emphasis on teamwork and quality consciousness.

The case of Toyota Auto Body, though sketchy, provides enough information to draw a number of fundamental conclusions about the characteristics of an organization with developed and successful quality circles.

A quality circle effort is large in scope. The fact that nearly three fourths of the employees of Toyota Auto Body participate in 841 circles, turning out roughly 1,800 successful projects each year, demonstrates that quality circles make a highly significant contribution to the regular organization.

Quality circles are permanent. Quality circles have existed at Toyota Auto Body for eighteen years. A successful quality circle process means a permanent change in the organization. When planning the installation of quality circles, we must think in decades, not years, and certainly not months.

The quality circle process is part of the in-line management process. Toyota Auto Body takes great care to ensure that quality circles work in harmony with middle management and supervision. Responsibility for training is placed among staff at the section level. Foremen, supervisors, and leaders who are not supervisors meet regularly to make sure that the objectives of everyone are compatible. In the early stage of quality circle growth and development, only supervisors became circle leaders. All these things ensure that middle managers and supervisors have a stake in the success of the quality circle process and do not separate themselves from it.

The organization provides the skills necessary for circles to be successful. It trains every employee in fundamental organizational, statistical, and problem-solving skills. It trains circle leaders in the fundamentals of small-group leadershp and shows them how to achieve consensus. And when the technical expertise needed exceeds the capacity of the organization to train, the organization makes a body of engineering knowledge available through the Industrial Engineering Project team. All this represents a profound commitment to giving circle members everything they need to succeed.

The organization provides incentives to encourage participation. Through monetary incentives such as the suggestion and bonus systems, Toyota Auto Body creates an environment in which individual employees, by their own voluntary actions, can increase their income and enhance their careers through participation in quality circles. The company also organizes competition between circles, in which prestige and recognition become additional incentives to encourage participation in quality circles. Thus rewards, monetary and otherwise, are more available to those who participate and less available to those who do not.

The organization creates controls to ensure that the quality circle process does not disrupt its ultimate objective. This characteristic is not especially visible in the case of Toyota Auto Body, but evidence does exist. The leader council sees to it that the goals of the organization and the goals of the circles are in harmony, or at least not in conflict. Training is provided to focus the circles on problems whose solution will aid the organization. Though they do not appear in the available information on Toyota Auto Body, there are undoubtedly rules for the operation of quality circles which define the outer limits of their activities. And the process of making the presentation to management, which provides full management review, in turn ensures ultimate management control.

The organization regularly evaluates itself to ensure that it and the quality circle process are on track. Most large organizations do some of this. Toyota Auto Body gives particular emphasis to the annual attitude survey as a means of tracking its organizational well-being.

The organization provides mechanisms to facilitate implementation of quality circle proposals that have been adopted. Though not explicitly described in information provided by Toyota Auto Body, the presence of interlocking offices, teams, and circles makes it clear that the organization is prepared to put proposals into effect quickly and efficiently.

Upper management is totally committed to quality circles. This characteristic is implicit in the entire description of quality circles at Toyota Auto Body. An effort which includes 72 percent of the employees, which involves offices and circles throughout the organizational hierarchy, and which necessitates a massive training and study program cannot succeed without full and unequivocal dedication by top management.

In summary, these nine characteristics provide a clear image of our objective. When fully installed, quality circles:

1. Encompass the entire organization from top to bottom.
2. Are permanent.
3. Are promoted, trained, and maintained by in-line management.

Further, the organization as a whole

4. Dedicates itself to continuous study of improvements in quality and productivity; trains personnel and provides technical expertise through the Industrial Engineering Project Team.
5. Provides an incentive structure that strongly favors participation in quality circles.
6. Provides the necessary bureaucratic mechanisms to implement quality circle proposals that are accepted.

7. Maintains control while the program develops.
8. Measures organizational results to ensure that the program is on track.

Finally, before anything can happen,

9. Upper management provides unwavering support.

In the following chapters, we turn our attention to a step-by-step plan for achieving these objectives.

PART TWO
Installing
Quality Circles

3

Installation:
What Can Go Wrong

The goal of an installation program is to make the quality circle process a permanent, self-sustaining part of the management process of your organization—to institutionalize it. The quality circle process is a *system* of management practice, not a program. To achieve it, you must take a great deal of care, spend a lot of time planning and preparing, and have uncommon amounts of patience and perseverance. You are trying to change an organization. A lot can go wrong.

In the course of installing quality circles, you will encounter many problems. Most are easily solved and do not require comment, but some are major. They are best described as pitfalls—deadly hidden traps along the trail. If you do not solve them before they appear—if you do not cut a safe trail—they can jeopardize your efforts, either putting an end to quality circles in your organization or leading to a final result entirely different from the permanent, self-sustaining quality circle process. These pitfalls are:

- Misunderstanding of the quality circle process by upper management.

ʞ • Resistance to quality circles by middle management and supervision.
ϰ • Poor training.
ϰ • Empire building by the quality circle office.
ϰ • Failure to implement circle proposals.
ϰ • Failure to measure results of the quality circle process.
ϒ • Quality circles that deviate from the basic structure described in this book.

Here is an example of a circle that failed after an initial success. It exemplifies many of the problems which, although they do not at first appear to be problems, can eventually cause a circle—and even the entire circle process—to fail.

CASE #3
The Wrong Way

The staff members of the quality circle office of a large manufacturing firm began forming circles before fully understanding all the elements necessary for a successful program. They failed to provide training courses for managers, supervisors, and leaders. They lacked a clear set of policies about quality circle structure and process, they had no formal program for measuring the impact of quality circles on the organization, and they had not foreseen the need to prepare the organization for dealing with the quality circle process. All they had was a vague notion of the quality circle concept and some basic training materials for members.

To form its first circles, the office advertised for volunteers through the company news bulletin. Shortly afterward, it was approached by a group of tool fabricators who wanted to form a circle in their area. They had terrible problems, and they wanted to do something about them.

The office was delighted and, over the next several days, held a series of meetings with them to work out the details.

It soon became clear that the fabricators disagreed with one aspect of the quality circle concept: they did not want a supervisor in their circle. The tool fabrication shop had a history of bad relations between supervisors and fabricators. Over the years it had acquired a reputation for being slow and unreliable. In frustration, the company began to send much of its work to outside vendors. Both supervisors and fabricators knew this and blamed each other. The supervisors berated the men as incompetent and lazy, blaming them for the poor reputation. The fabricators, in turn, felt that the supervisors and management were to blame and harassed the supervisors whenever they could.

The quality circle office worked hard to convince the fabricators that the process would work more effectively with a supervisor in the circle, but the fabricators stubbornly refused to form a circle that way. Finally the office relented. A circle without a supervisor seemed better than no circle at all.

There were other, less visible, problems with the tool fabricators' circle. Its members came from different areas within the tool fabrication shop and worked for different supervisors. In effect, the circle was formed from a network of friends that cut across the formal organization of the shop. They had volunteered—no one had forced them. But on the other hand, other fabricators in the shop had not been invited to join.

From the very first meeting it was clear that the circle would have trouble with supervisors in the tool fabrication shop. The supervisors resented the loss of control over one hour per week of the fabricators' time. They refused to let some of the men go to the meeting, and the office had to step in and force them to do so. The following week the same thing happened and, once again, the office had to intervene, this time with a memo reminding the supervisors of the importance given quality circles by the plant manager.

Once the quality circle office established the right to hold the meeting, the advisor from the quality circle office trained the fabricators, and then they turned to their first project. They chose the problem of excessive defects discovered on tools fabricated by outside vendors. This selection disturbed the advisor, who felt that the problem was too difficult to tackle initially because its origins lay outside the shop, the department, and even the company. It sounded too ambitious. Better, he argued, to choose a simple problem within the shop as their first project. He lost the argument.

The circle proceeded to investigate defects on tools produced outside the plant. As they progressed, the advisor began to grasp the significance of their choice. Vendors produced poor tools. The tools were inspected at the vendor's plant, but most defects escaped the cursory check by inspectors. Once in-house, the tools were again inspected, but carelessly. The defects quickly surfaced when the tools were in use, and it became the tool fabricators' responsibility to make repairs. But because the system for reporting discrepancies was inadequate, the tool fabricators were credited with the defects. In short, they were being blamed for defective tools that they did not produce. At least, that is how the fabricators saw it. They admitted that in the past their shop had done shoddy work. But now, they claimed, they had improved considerably. They did not deserve the bad reputation that hounded them, and they wanted a chance to prove themselves. This, then, was the motivation behind their project.

In the course of their investigation, the members discovered that the system for reporting discrepancies had more flaws than they had suspected. A computer run on defects charged to the vendors revealed a negligible amount, far less than firsthand experience suggested. Thus, as their first solution, the tool fabrication quality circle chose to redesign the defect-reporting system to document the origin of each defect especially those produced by outside vendors. They designed a new defect tag for inspectors to complete and a new tool change notice to request that defects be repaired. Finally, they coordinated with the computer staff to systematically store and retrieve data.

After months of research and preparation, the circle gave its presentation. It was the first ever by a quality circle at the plant. It went well. The members sounded articulate and forceful. Management was impressed by their figures and quickly approved the new system for monitoring defects. The discussion period lasted over an hour and provided enough interchange for the circle members to become recognizable personalities to upper management.

The members were ecstatic. From their point of view they had vindicated themselves before the world, and especially before their supervisors. Of the two, the latter was more important. Prior to the presentation, supervisors had taunted the members, claiming that they would never get their proposal accepted and would make fools of themselves. The members had not only proved themselves, but they had established friendly and open rapport with the highest ranking people in the organization. They had, in short, outflanked the supervisors.

Over the next couple of months, as work progressed on their second project, some of the members began to harass the supervisors. Whenever pushed or hassled, they reminded the supervisors of their success and close relationship with upper management. The implication was clear. They could and would report the supervisors' incompetence and inadequacy to upper management if the supervisors failed to do the members' bidding.

It was an effective tactic. The supervisors believed that the members had the power to act on the threat, and they feared for their jobs. To a degree, they had reason to be fearful. The shop's reputation for being poorly run meant that supervision and middle management lived in a constant state of defensive anxiety.

The tool fabrication quality circle's second project developed out of the first. The circle decided that the only way to put an end to the problem of defective tools arriving undetected was to go to the vendors and inspect them before shipment. The quality department was already doing this, of course, but the circle argued that the field inspectors were not qualified to inspect welds and high-tolerance dimensions. In fact, they surmised that the field representatives were just "buying paper"—that is, making sure that the paperwork was in order.

Their proposed solution was simple. They suggested that a special team, composed of hourly tool fabricators, be sent to a vendor just before shipment of a major tool. Together with the field inspector, they would inspect the tool and report all defects back to him for a decision on acceptance or rejection. The team would usurp no one's job, nor would it require a new job category.

The supervisors openly told the members that they would never obtain approval. They called them troublemakers and malcontents. They insisted that the circle members were really after the inspectors' jobs. In short, the supervisors' envy, resentment, and fear continued to increase.

Contrary to their prediction, management accepted the proposal. Within a month the first team visited a vendor, inspected a tool, and discovered defects. By order of the inspector, the vendor repaired the tool before shipping it. The new procedure worked very well.

The success of this project exacerbated the conflict in the tool fabrication shop. The circle members tormented the supervisors with their success and especially their apparent chumminess with upper management. This "link to the top" was visibly brought home when the plant manager visited the shop and personally spoke to the members.

As a third project, the circle decided to attack the major problem in their area: the organization of the work process itself. The shop moved through cycles of too much work followed by too little work, primarily because, the members felt, the system for establishing work schedules was weak. Moreover, the fabricators were constantly being given inadequate tools, materials, or plans to complete a job, and as a result, the storage area was cluttered with half-finished jobs.

Their analysis showed that the major problem was organizational. The tool fabrication shop did not control its own destiny. Schedules and supplies were handled within another hierarchy, the tool control office. This, the members reasoned, made it virtually impossible for the tool fabrication shop to operate efficiently.

This was not a new analysis. A number of middle managers had recognized the problem for some time, but had been unable to win approval to change the system. The circle contacted these managers and proposed an alliance. The success of the previous projects made it clear that the quality circle process was an effective means to bring about change in a bureaucracy that otherwise proved immovable. The managers accepted the alliance and worked closely with the circle members in developing a solution.

This project had one major difficulty. It constituted an attack on the competence of the tool control office and, in particular, the general foreman of that office. As the circle attempted to collect data to show the number of jobs that were set in motion without the necessary materials, as well as the number of times the entire shop lay idle—even though there was an ample backlog—the tool control office became more and more agitated. In the rumor networks of the plant, the general foreman claimed that he was being personally attacked and that the circle was trying to have him fired. His supervisors felt the same way. Even though the tool fabrication supervisors had reason to agree with the circle's point of view, the controversy further fed their fears that the existence of the circle threatened their authority and perhaps even their jobs. They could easily identify with the tool control supervisors. Moreover, they felt that all along they had been an indirect target of the group's activities. They were sure that next time they would be the direct target.

The situation put the advisor in a tough spot. In each regular meeting, he attempted to convince the circle members to use great tact. They could, he argued, win their case and improve the shop without deepening the rift between themselves and the supervisors. His words had little effect. Without involvement of tool fabrication supervisors in quality circle activities, and especially without a supervisor participating in the circle, his efforts to control their behavior made him appear to be no more than an enforcer. The members quickly transferred the hostility they felt for supervisors to the advisor. They engaged him in bitter arguments. They accused him of selling out to management. They even turned the argument around and threatened to go to management with the accusation that the advisor was trying to block their project. His ability to influence their behavior plummeted, and by the time of the presentation, he had lost all their trust. They had not shown him copies of their pitch, and he literally had no idea what they were going to propose. In effect, the circle was out of control.

The presentation was a tense affair. The director of manufacturing attended with all his managers, as well as the general foremen and supervisors from tool fabrication and tool control. The circle members went through their analysis of the problem and their proposed solution—a reorganization of both shops that would put key control in the hands of tool fabrication so that it could effectively schedule its work. The director listened.

When they finished their pitch, they opened the meeting for comments and discussion. But the director assumed control of the meeting and announced that there would be no discussion. Instead, he would appoint a committee to look into the matter and report back to the circle. Attempts by a few of the managers to discuss the proposal were pointedly suppressed by the director. He was firm—there would be no discussion.

Before the meeting adjourned, the director developed a list of people to serve on the committee. It included several supervisors from both the tool fabrication and tool control shops and one member of the circle—the youngest and least experienced. Clearly the director was attempting to whitewash the problem and bury the report.

The circle members were confused at first, then furious. In their next regular meeting they agreed that they had been treated badly. The director had refused to abide by even the most basic rule of the quality circle process: a free and open discussion of the proposal. They realized that he was attempting to whitewash the issue, but they felt powerless. Their only option was to disband until he reported back to them. They were convinced that he never would, but somehow they wanted to make the point that he was violating the rules of the quality circle process.

Both the advisor and his boss, the quality circle program administrator, spoke with the director on numerous occasions, urging him to respond personally to the circle as soon as possible. He did not, and it became clear that he would not. Although much of his resistance stemmed from a lack of understanding of the quality circle process, he was also acting out of what he felt to be political necessity. As he phrased it, "I've got a shop full of supervisors terrified of their employees. They are truly scared for their jobs." In short, he felt that his only choice, in view of the hostility in the shop, was to squash the circle and openly support the supervisors.

The circle's activity came to a complete halt. Given the lead by the director, supervisors in the tool fabrication area took the offensive. They transferred members to different locations around the plant and divided the group. They circulated rumors to the effect that the two most active members of the circle would be "set up" and fired. One member claimed to have received a threat to that effect.

In the face of this attack, the members reaffirmed their decision to disband. But there was more to their final decision than just the struggle with the supervisors. The members themselves had come to disagree about the role of quality circles and the tactics they, as circle members, should employ. The more vocal and aggressive minority favored keeping supervisors out of the circle and engaging in direct, confrontation politics. The majority, less vocal, felt that in the long run more cooperation and less confrontation would serve them better. They wanted supervisors to participate. When the time came to decide on disbanding permanently, the majority registered its vote more as a matter of exhaustion with confrontation politics than as defeat.

The Tool Fabrication Quality Circle never reformed. A year later, however, after receiving extensive training in leading a quality circle, two of the supervisors from the tool fabrication shop formed successful and enduring quality circles.

• • •

You can avoid the major pitfalls of quality circle installation by following these five steps, in order, with care and patience.

1. Obtain upper management support and commitment, and establish a quality circle office to promote the quality circle process throughout the organization.
2. Develop a logical strategy for forming circles on the basis of a clear understanding of the pitfalls and of the long-term goal: to make quality circles a permanent, self-sustaining part of the management process.
3. Promote within the organization the systems that are necessary to support the quality circle process.
4. Prepare training programs for all members of the organization.
5. Work out all the details, from acquiring a meeting room to codifying the rules of the quality circle process.

You should not form your first circle until you consider *all* these steps. If you start circles before all the elements are in place, you may end up with one like the tool fabrication group.

The following chapters present the issues and options of each of these five steps.

4

Institutionalizing the Quality Circle Office

Before you can install quality circles, you must obtain approval. But from whom? The answer is obvious—from upper management. Nothing less will do. A quality circle effort requires the active participation of the entire organization if it is to succeed. This means that top management must be fully and completely aware of and behind the effort.

Attempting to install quality circles in a single department without upper management knowledge or approval will produce predictable calamities. They will encounter resistance and fail because the supporters of the program are powerless to overcome opposition or negotiate a compromise. Or, when the program has failed to receive proper guidance, it will encounter problems that thrust it into the awareness of upper management in a negative light.

CASE #4
Proceeding Without Approval from the Top

The director of quality control in a midwestern manufacturing company decided to promote quality circles from within his department without the knowledge of the company executive or other department directors. He wanted to experiment. If quality circles turned out to be a success, he would unveil them. If not, then nothing was lost.

Unfortunately, he could afford only one man to work with the circles. Lacking office guidance and support from the entire organization, this one man could not get the help he needed to build the best possible quality circle process. As the number of circles grew, he exerted less and less control. Soon circles were involved in a wide range of projects and problems, and some began to work on highly sensitive issues such as wages, grievances, and job classifications. This eventually attracted attention and brought a full-scale investigation by the executive into "whatever is going on down there in quality?"

Involving the Union

If your organization has a union, it is imperative that you include it in quality circles from the very start. Contact and consult with a union representative at every step. If possible, place one on a steering committee.

The union is crucial for both philosophical and practical reasons. With respect to the former, quality circles depend on cooperation and mutual benefit. They simply do not work in an atmosphere heavily laden with mistrust and antagonism. Thus, whatever the history of union relations at your organization, you should make every effort to establish a partnership between union and management. From a practical standpoint, if you do not bring the union into your plans from the very beginning, it may turn against quality circles for no other reason than that the concept was proposed by management. If involved in the planning, however, the union will find it advantageous to take a constructive stance toward quality circles.

A warning: Neither union nor management should

promote quality circles through the contract. Placing quality circles in the context of adversarial bargaining contradicts the spirit of joint effort and partnership. When part of a contract, quality circles inevitably become a bargaining point, with each side placing conditions on it. Even when quality circles are kept out of contract negotiations, an adversarial approach often undermines the first steps in the quality circle's development.

CASE #5
Settling Old Scores

A small chemicals firm in the South heard of quality circles and began to investigate the concept. An assistant to the plant manager visited various companies where quality circles were in operation. He saw nothing but outstanding success and reported to his boss that their firm should move as fast as possible to set up its own program.

The local union, however, posed a problem. For the last few years the local president had led the members in a bitter and acrimonious dispute over chemical contamination of employees. He claimed, with some evidence, that as many as 65 percent of the union members had sustained liver damage because of the company's negligence. The issue had reached such intensity that on certain occasions physical violence had erupted between the president of the union and the director of industrial relations.

Given this atmosphere of mistrust, there seemed little hope of starting quality circles, but the assistant was patient and determined. After a series of false starts, he persuaded the union president to visit a factory that had circles in operation. After receiving a formal presentation on quality circles, the president talked to circle members on the shop floor and questioned them about the relationship between their union and quality circles.

The experience dispelled all his fears that the circles and the union would be at odds. He returned to his members, convinced that they should support quality circles. Unfortunately, he also decided that the situation offered an opportunity to settle the contamination issue. He reasoned that, if the company wanted quality circles badly enough, it would admit to the contamination problem and provide compensation. He placed such a condition on the union's acceptance of quality circles.

The assistant to the plant manager would not be bullied. He knew that the company would not recognize the contamination issue. He also recognized that quality circles would not work if conditions were placed on them. From his point of view, either management and the union would join together on unconditional terms or they would not do it at all. Over several weeks he argued the issues with the union president and eventually convinced him to drop the contamination issue.

It was clear, however, that though the union no longer regarded the contamination issue as a formal condition, most of the union officers looked to quality circles to solve the problem. They planned to bring it up through the quality circle process and force management to confront it. They were still putting a condition on the project, though more subtly—either the quality circle process solved the problem in their favor or they would judge quality circles a failure.

It should be added that the company was also placing expectations on quality circles. It hoped that somehow the quality circle process—systematic study of the problem by a small group of employees (not the union) and formal presentation of a solution (rather than an accusation and a demand or threat)—would defuse the issue.

The company and the union finally installed quality circles. It remains to be seen whether they will succeed.

Choosing a Consultant

It is not necessary to hire a consultant before developing a quality circle program. Given time and resources, you can (and should) take the following steps yourself. First, study the available literature and visit organizations with operating quality circles. Then you must sell the concept to management. Develop an installation strategy, prepare the organization by setting up systems to implement circle proposals and measure results of circle activities, write training materials, and work out the rules of the quality circle process for your organization. Finally, you can begin to form and train circles. Even with a consultant, you will eventually do all these things yourself if quality circles are to become a permanent, self-sustaining process in your organization. Success or failure is your responsibility, not the consultant's. Still, it is useful to have good advice and counsel, especially in the beginning. Moreover, a consultant can help you save time and avoid hassles in preparing training materials. Best of all, a consultant may keep you from making irrevocable mistakes.

The problem, of course, is how to choose a good consultant. The recent explosion of interest in quality circles has hatched a new breed of instant experts. Most haven't the slightest notion of what quality circles are all about, and very few have any actual experience with quality circles. After hearing a lecture, attending a seminar, or reading an article, they feel qualified to pose as experts. Their advise has been followed with sometimes devastating results.

Choosing a competent consultant should not be difficult. Simply take care and time to check the background of the prospective professional to make sure the following criteria are met. A qualified consultant:

- Has worked directly in the promotion, training, and advising of twenty or more quality circles (beyond the pilot program stage).
- Has been involved in quality circles for more than two years.
- Can provide you with training materials (manuals, workbooks, slides).
- Is willing to spend at least a week at your organization training the first circle leaders and the first circles as well as advisors and trainers if necessary.
- Will remain available indefinitely to answer questions and help solve problems that arise.

These are the minimum requirements. In the best relationship, the consultant would make regular visits to your organization to hold training sessions and evaluate the progress of the installation program. This relationship should endure for two to three years.

Explaining the Concept

Once you have determined who should approve the concept, the next step is to explain it. This is a crucial undertaking. The experience of most managers does not prepare them to understand the quality circle process, but at the same time it steers them toward a number of misinterpretations. If they misunderstand the concept, they may reject it; just as bad, they may approve it without understanding what they are getting into.

To explain the concept, prepare a formal presentation using the information in Chapters 1 and 2. For additional information, contact the International Association of Quality Circles, the American Society for Quality Control, and any other organizations promoting quality circles in the United States. Look into videotapes and slide sets on the subject of quality circles. Several are available.

When you give the pitch to management, take your time. Do not try to do it all in one sitting. Bring in someone to speak on quality circles who has had firsthand experience. Above all, try to arrange for managers to visit organizations with functioning quality circles. Best of all, have them attend a circle meeting and a management presentation.

Be prepared for the fact that most managers—and, indeed, almost everyone in your organization—will probably misinterpret the concept at first. Here are some examples of common misconceptions.

A temporary cure: Almost everyone initially regards the quality circle process as a short-term project lasting no longer than six or nine months. They see a quality circle as a technique that one prescribes, like medicine, to cure an ill, such as poor quality or low productivity. Once the disease is cured, they reason, the organization can stop taking the medicine.

A limited endeavor: Most managers imagine that the quality circle process is a minor undertaking, involving only the shops or offices where they are having trouble. They see, at most, only 10 or 15 percent of the work force participating.

A one-problem solution: Managers usually decide that the quality circle process does only one thing. More correctly, they want it to do only one specific job. They want simplicity. The job may be to save money, improve quality, raise productivity, or reduce turnover. Whatever the problem, they limit themselves to one target.

For employees only: Managers see the quality circle process as changing the work force but not the organization. From their point of view, it changes employees but not managers.

Just a program: Underlying and encompassing all of these misinterpretations is the notion that quality circles constitute a program. This usage has subtle implications. It makes quality circles an *encapsulated addition* to the organization—something with a beginning and an end that never really becomes part of the organization itself and only involves a limited number of people in the resolution of a specific problem.

To counteract these misconceptions, you should encourage managers to see the quality circle process for what it really is—a management practice or system. It changes the way managers manage by changing the very nature of the relationships among employees themselves and between employees and their supervisors and managers. The process requires managers to support participation in quality circles actively and persistently. Above all, it requires them to listen seriously to their employees and respond in good faith to their proposals and requests. As such, it is a large undertaking that involves the entire organization, especially managers. And it takes time—years, not months—to install. But once in place, the process improves the entire output of the organization simultaneously, from employee productivity to product quality, and keeps improving it forever.

CASE #6
Nothing But a Fancy Suggestion System

When a division of a large aerospace company decided to install quality circles, the director of industrial relations was against it. As far as he was concerned, it was little more than a glorified suggestion system, and the company already had one of those. What, he demanded, could quality circles do that a good suggestion system could not do more cheaply?

The proponents of quality circles had very little concrete evidence to offer in response. The concept was new and few American companies had tried it. The Japanese figures showed dramatic results in such things as employee morale and productivity, but their figures were very general and there was no information on how they were obtained. The proponents could only assert that they believed that quality circles would have a tremendously positive impact on the organization, although they couldn't prove it. Fortunately, most of the directors and the plant manager wanted to try it. Despite lack of hard evidence, they decided to go ahead.

Over the next year and a half, the number of active circles slowly increased and the evidence of the positive impact of their activities mounted. The director of industrial relations began to see that quality circles were doing something for the organization that a suggestion system could never accomplish. In fact, when his own question was repeated at a presentation to visiting corporate vice presidents, he answered it.

"First," he said, "quality circles promote teamwork and cooperation, while a suggestion system promotes competition and conflict. Both encourage employees to think of better ways to do a job, but the suggestion system provokes people to work against one another for an award. It actually discourages them from discussing an idea and putting their heads together to improve on it. The rush to get the idea submitted first and win the award causes conflict, and we don't need more conflict in our organization. Quality circles, in contrast, promote group cooperation, group solutions, and group rewards.

"Second, quality circles do a great deal that suggestion systems do not do. They both produce cost-saving ideas, but quality circles have a huge impact on the organization as a whole. They raise employee productivity. They reduce quality defects. They reduce turnover, absenteeism, and lost time. They reduce accidents. A suggestion system can't do any of these things.

"Most of all, quality circles involve hourly employees in the decisions of the company, at least those that relate to the shop floor. We've never done this before, but it works."

Winning Approval and Commitment

Winning approval should be easy. There are enough selling points with quality circles for at least one of them to catch the attention of even the most unsympathetic manager. Indeed, your major problem is to sell quality circles without overselling them. There is always the temptation to imply that quality circles will buy something for nothing. They will not. It costs money to install quality circles. It costs money to maintain them. And over the years it will cost money to sustain them. Granted, the return far exceeds the investment, but, as with everything else, it takes money to make money.

Winning a commitment from management is far more difficult than winning approval. Managers can state their commitment, but until they prove it under fire, you never know whether you really have their unconditional support or not.

The only thing you can do to help build a commitment that will stand the test of time is to present managers with all the information you possibly can about quality circles. Follow the rule of "no surprises." Show them all the benefits, but also show them the problems. Present the Toyota Auto Body example in Chapter 2 so that they realize the magnitude and permanence of a quality circle effort. Acquaint managers with the types of problems that you will encounter and the solutions you will undertake. Above all, do not hold back under the mistaken notion that they would not agree to install quality circles if they knew the difficulties. This approach will eventually hurt you. It will create false expectations and an inevitable loss of support and commitment when difficulties arise.

Institutionalizing Sponsorship

Once management makes the decision to go ahead with quality circles, the next step is to find a sponsor for the program. The immediate temptation, and a dangerous error, is to hand it over to an existing department. Don't do it! Quality circles require the support and participation of the entire organization from the start. The organization as a whole must sponsor the effort.

One means of promoting organizational sponsorship is to form a steering committee, composed of top-level representatives from each major department in the organization and any office whose special skills are useful in installation. The steering committee might include the plant manager, directors of major departments such as manufacturing, quality, and engineering, as well as representatives from training, public relations, and industrial relations.

A steering committee serves the following purposes:

- It institutionalizes permanent, broad, top-level support for the quality circle effort. Quality circles that are sponsored by only one person, such as the plant manager, are likely to be destroyed by his death or transfer.
- It promotes a broad sense of ownership by involving all the major departments. Every department can see

the quality circle effort as its own, rather than "just something they're doing over in industrial relations." At the very least, the sponsoring departments cannot oppose it.

- It serves as the initial focus of a campaign to educate the entire organization about quality circles. For example, you or your consultant can make a presentation to the committee on the quality circle process. The committee members, in turn, can arrange to give the same presentation to key people in their departments.

- It oversees the entire installation program and the activities of the quality circle office. Specifically, it should set installation goals and timetables for the quality circle office, as well as make major policy decisions as installation takes place.

Forming a steering committee is an optional step. The same functions can be fulfilled in the regular staff meeting of the plant manager and his directors, and this approach has the advantage of making quality circles a part of regular business, which is what they are and always should be. On the other hand, a steering committee helps to highlight the program and emphasize it so that it is not lost in the regular business of the staff meeting.

There are two ways to go about forming a steering committee. You can ask that executive management sit as a committee, with assistance from other departments, as already suggested. Or you can form a steering committee of volunteers, drawn from whatever levels and departments within the organization wish to participate. The two approaches require different treatment.

An executive steering committee will only review what the quality circle office does and will issue directives concerning the circle office's policies. The object is to keep executive management well informed about the progress of installation and sold on the worth of quality circles in general. A volunteer steering committee, on the other hand, needs to be told what to do. The major cause for failure among steering committees of this type is that the members are asked to "steer" without being told what that means. Therefore, have the members of the committee meet to draft a proposal for measuring the impact of the quality circle process on the organization. Have the committee work closely with the administrator of the quality circle office, when it is formed, to write, review, and accept a strategy and schedule for installing quality circles in the organization. As it gains experience and understanding, the committee can begin to establish the rules and procedures for making presentations to management, ensuring implementation of proposals, and so on.

There is a third alternative worth considering. Do not form a steering committee until you have formed quality circles. Each time a department attains a significant level of participation in circles, have a representative—volunteer or appointee—join the steering committee to help with additional circle promotion, technical support to circles, project follow-up, and interdepartmental coordination.

Our discussion so far refers to a single organization. Frequently, however, a number of separate organizations at different locations are targets of a single quality circle effort. For example, the corporate offices or headquarters of a company may seek to promote quality circles among its various divisions, and these divisions may, in turn, seek to promote them at each manufacturing or office location. Or a city government may want to promote quality circles in all its offices and agencies, from tax collection to sanitation. In cases like these, steering committees can serve as a means of linking organizations. Within a large corporation, for example, each facility might have its own steering committee with representation on the divisional steering committee. In similar fashion, the divisional steering committee would have representatives on the corporate steering committee.

A warning: Interlocking steering committees of the kind just mentioned coordinate and facilitate communication between organizations, but they fail if they are used as chains of command. In fact, one organization cannot expect to impose quality circles on another organization through steering committees or any other means, be it corporate headquarters or city hall. Each organization—meaning a single physical location in which people interact in a hierarchical structure—must own its quality circle effort. If forced into it by outside edict, the effort will very likely fail.

Institutionalizing Responsibility

One office should be charged with the specific responsibility of installing quality circles. Success depends on a vigorous and continuous effort that can be sustained only by an in-house agency, an office devoted exclusively to the tasks of writing an installation plan, getting it approved by a steering committee and/or upper management, implementing it, modifying it when necessary, and seeing that the plan becomes an integral part of the organization.

It is possible to conceive of installation programs without a central quality circle office. A consultant might train all the managers and all the supervisors and then turn them loose in the organization with the expectation that they will perform as trained, while he moves on to his next client. Or the corporate offices might attempt to perform the same consulting role. In either case, however, the odds are against the effort succeeding.

People do not behave "as trained." A quality circle process involves changing some of the behavior of almost everyone in the organization—managers, supervisors, and employees. These changes do not occur overnight. People must be advised and guided in their new roles over a long period of time. To do this, you need an office in the organization that can act as a permanent consultant, trainer, and advisor to everyone struggling to understand the quality circle process and how to perform successfully within it.

Furthermore, despite careful planning, promotion, and training, some managers and supervisors will resist quality circles. They will do so actively and vocally, or they will do so surreptitiously. In some cases, they may even try to sabotage quality circles. When resistance or sabotage occurs, there must be an office capable of detecting and responding to it immediately and vigorously.

Locating the Quality Circle Office

Having established the need for a central quality circle office, the next step is to designate its location within the organization. This is crucial, as a poorly positioned office can cause difficulties. If placed too low in the hierarchy, it may lack the clout needed to fulfill its functions. If placed in the wrong department, it may become too closely identified with the particular interests of that department.

The location of quality circle offices within organizations varies considerably around the United States. Many place it within the department responsible for quality control, assuming because of its name that it belongs there. Others place it in the personnel or industrial relations department and classify it under "human resource management" or something similar. Still other organizations place it in the manufacturing division.

Although manufacturing is the most logical location, all these choices have a major drawback. Sooner or later, the quality circle process will involve the entire organization. If quality circles are identified with one particular department, other departments may aggressively or covertly resist it, or at least regard it as an unavoidable nuisance. It will always remain, to some extent, "their" program, not "ours."

CASE #7
In the Quality Control Department

In an assembly facility of a large aerospace firm, the quality circle office was located in the quality control department. As circles formed, advisors encountered resistance, sporadic at first, then persistent, among manufacturing personnel. With time, it became clear that the quality control inspectors and manufacturing employees were in such a hostile, adversary relationship that it was affecting the circles. The manufacturing people saw the quality circle advisor as a kind of spy, an agent of the quality control department, and his presence stifled discussion. They felt that the advisors, who attended all meetings, would help the inspectors "come down" on them. They feared that whatever was said about quality problems in the meetings would eventually appear in a discrepancy report.

The advisors continually tried to convince the manufacturing personnel that they stood above these interdepartmental rivalries, but to no avail. They could not win their trust. The situation remained the same, crippling the quality circle effort, until the office was transferred to the staff of the plant manager.

• • •

Another important consideration is the resistance by some managers and supervisors. Despite complete dissemination of information about the quality circle process, as well as extensive training and guidance for management, there will always be a few people who will resist the program once they begin to experience it. A supervisor might find ways to keep employees from attending circle meetings, or a director might stifle discussion in a management presentation and retreat behind closed doors to make a decision unilaterally. To deal with these situations, the quality circle office must have the power and influence to force the supervisor and the director to abide by the rules of the quality circle process.

The only logical way to meet these needs is to attach the quality circle office to the staff of the plant manager. (See Diagram 5.) Here it can function "over" the entire organization, independent of the particular interests of each department. Moreover, it has access to the highest authority of the organization, so that when necessary, it can "enforce" the rules. In short, placing the office on the plant manager's staff gives the quality circle office the organizational clout to succeed.

Organizing the Office

A quality circle office has three essential positions: program administrator, trainer, and advisor.

Program administrator: The program administrator bears overall responsibility for the installation program. The administrator writes the installation plan and sees that it is carried out, hires one or more trainers and advisors to assist in this process, manages their activities, and reports to the steering committee and executive management. The

DIAGRAM 5

Location of the quality circle office.

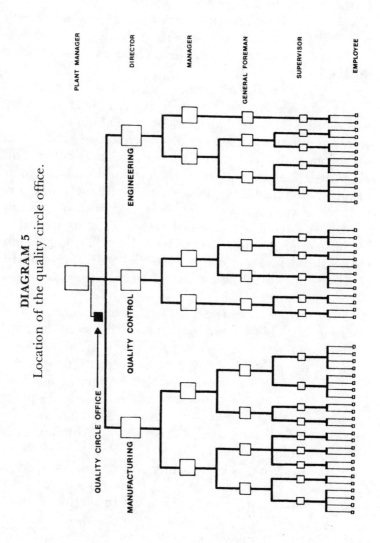

administrator acts as troubleshooter and enforces the rules of the quality circle process.

Trainer: The trainer prepares and carries out training courses for managers, supervisor-leaders, employee-members, and advisors on their respective roles in the quality circle process.

Advisor: The advisor advises quality circles, and particularly circle leaders, on how to run their meetings, solve problems, and make management presentations. The advisor attends all the meetings of the circles assigned to him or her, meets privately with the circle leaders before and after their meetings to help organize and evaluate their progress, and provides minor logistical support in the way of viewgraphs, room arrangements, and memos. The advisor keeps detailed records of each circle's progress and mediates and attempts to solve problems arising within circles and between circles and the wider organization. In short, the advisor is the action arm of the installation program.

Most people apply the title "facilitator" to what I have just described. I have chosen not to use that word, because I think it obscures and mystifies the role. Indeed, the mystification undoubtedly explains why so many people are fond of the term. The mystery makes them seem more professional. This tendency is worsened by the frequent application of "facilitator" to program administrators, trainers, and advisors, as well as a variety of combinations of those several positions.

In the early stages of installing a program, you should not overstaff a quality circle office. One person, the program administrator, is sufficient to get through the planning stage. However, as soon as the time approaches to begin training people, you should acquire additional personnel, perhaps someone to double as trainer and advisor.

Eventually, as the number of circles grows, you will need more people.

Whatever combination of roles you create, it is important to recognize that two of them—program administrator and advisor—work better when kept separate. Though distinct, they complement each other. The program administrator is management oriented and deals primarily with executive management, working to keep the office funded, staffed, and advancing. The advisor, on the other hand, must build strong rapport with circle leaders and circle members. He must be employee oriented. The administrator needs the advisor to work with circles as a trusted equal of employees. The advisor needs the administrator to serve as the ultimate authority on program policy and to intervene at higher management levels.

CASE #8
Saying No!

Frank, an advisor, works with a group of machinists who have been around a long time. They feel that they know what is happening and why. When they formed a circle, they immediately began to test the limits of their new powers as circle members. Once they settled on a project—reorganization of the flow of work through their area—they began to demand more time to work on it than the rules of the program allowed. The circle argued rather persuasively that time spent on the project was more important than time spent on their regular work. Feeling somewhat cowed by his men and still unsure of his role in the circle, the supervisor deflected the demand to the advisor, the spokesman for the quality circle office.

This put Frank on the spot. He had spent two months establishing rapport with the machinists in order to guide them toward a successful conclusion of their project. He had learned their personalities, learned their lingo, and won their trust. They viewed him as one of them. Now the situation called for a complete reversal. It demanded that Frank assume authority and become a representative of management policing their activities. To avoid direct confrontation, Frank told the circle that he would like them to have more time, but the rules of the quality circle process—an abstraction over which he had no control—forbade it. The machinists were not to be daunted. They demanded more time and threatened to quit the circle if they did not get it.

Frank's position now became critical. He had to maintain his relationship with the members in order to have any influence over them at all. He had to appear to be with them on this issue, or at least to be viewed as a friendly adversary. He could not assume the role of authority and make the final judgment against them without losing their trust. He needed an authority to back him up and to play the heavy.

To resolve this dilemma, Frank turned to Al, the program administrator. Al attended the next regular meeting of the circle, listened to their arguments and entreaties, sympathized with their desire to reorganize their shop, and then calmly denied their request in a formal statement of company policy on the matter. Until such time as the rules are altered, he told them, they would function only within the specified time.

This worked well. The machinists grumbled and complained, but continued with their circle and completed their project. Al took the heat as the villain. Frank maintained his working relationships.

CASE #9
Dealing with Big Shots

A circle composed of draftsmen and young engineers approached completion of the preparations for a management presentation concerning the reorganization of the drawing reproduction system. Their proposed solution was as complex and expensive as the problem, involving the entire engineering department as well as the reproduction and graphic support groups.

Suddenly the group learned that the manager of their section had developed a similar proposal. Apparently he got wind of their ideas and, out of embarrassment for not having done something about the problem sooner, or from sheer aggressiveness, planned to preempt their presentation and steal their thunder. The circle, needless to say, was dismayed. In good faith it had set out to solve a problem, and now one of their bosses hoped to take credit for it.

The advisor, Jan, was reluctant to approach the manager on this issue. He outranked her, and could simply say that he had known of the problem all along and had decided to take the necessary corrective measures. Jan chose instead to ask her boss, the program administrator, to speak to the manager and warn him not to make his presentation until after, and in response to, the circle's presentation. As a person of higher rank, and as the representative of the entire quality circle office, he could do so with greater effect. The program administrator went to the manager, and without making an accusation, politely pointed out that the quality circle's project was well known to everyone in the organization, including the manager's boss. If the manager were to give a presentation in advance of the circle's presentation, it would look as if he had tried to upstage the circle and he could find himself in an embarrassing position. The manager moved quickly to cancel his presentation and support the efforts of the quality circle.

• • •

The size of the staff of a quality circle office, and the question of whether to use trainers and advisors or just trainers, depends on the installation strategy. The next chapter addresses this issue.

5

Strategies
and Implementation

Too many program administrators forge ahead, once they receive approval to start, without giving thought to an ultimate objective or how to reach it. Hoping to learn by experience, they form a few circles and proceed on a day-to-day basis. Some—those with a great deal of luck and bureaucratic savvy—manage to survive. Most do not. Dozens of minor obstacles and one or more of the major pitfalls overwhelm them.

A more reasonable approach is to take the time to define the goal and then develop a strategy for achieving it *before* forming your first circle. As with many other endeavors, haste and lack of planning can lead you to disaster.

Defining the Goals

Of the nine characteristics of a successful quality circle effort at Toyota Auto Body, three relate directly to the formation of circles. Quality circles encompass the total organization, are permanent, and are promoted, trained, and maintained by in-line management. These characteristics are the objectives of a strategy to form quality circles. Their importance is best understood by considering what happens when they are not achieved.

It is almost impossible to install quality circles without eventually encompassing the entire organization. Vertically, the quality circle process requires both management and employees. Circle members define problems, analyze their causes, and propose solutions; management determines the acceptability of the solutions and initiates their implementation. Horizontally, an organization cannot limit circles to one functional area once they begin to produce visible results. Other employees will demand that they, too, have circles in their areas, and so will their management.

The quality circle office must make the process a permanent part of the organization. It will have failed if the organization suffers economically and management decides to drop quality circles, or if the program depends so heavily on a few key individuals that their death or transfer means the demise of the process.

Promoting, training, and maintaining quality circles permanently throughout the entire organization is really a question of ownership. If in-line management does not eventually "own" quality circles in this sense, then only two alternatives remain. Either the quality circle office owns the circles and becomes, in time, a burdensome bureaucracy that parallels and competes with in-line management, or no one takes over ownership and the process falters and dies.

Choosing a Strategy

There are two commonly used strategies for forming quality circles in any organization: *top-down* and *bottom-up*. In a top-down strategy, the quality circle office prepares, educates, and organizes (in that order) upper and middle management, supervisors, and, finally, employees. It assumes that you cannot successfully promote quality circles without first creating a receptive environment among managers. Since all power emanates from the top, conversion begins among managers and moves down the ranks. In this approach, quality circles are formed last.

In a bottom-up strategy, the opposite occurs. This philosophy assumes that management as a whole does not change "in a classroom." Rather, only experience forces change. Thus, in a bottom-up approach, circles are formed first. The various levels of management then learn to deal with the new politics of the organization through real-world encounters with circle presentations.

Each of these strategies has certain disadvantages. In the bottom-up approach, circle members receive a great deal of training and encouragement. They are told that if they follow the prescribed problem-solving techniques and present logical, documented, and economically feasible proposals, management will applaud their effort and implement the idea. However, management that has not been trained does not know anything about participative problem solving and has no idea how to receive a serious proposal from employees without feeling threatened. On the contrary, the vast majority of managers—consciously or unconsciously—strongly resist listening to employees. Few respond reasonably and positively. In fact, management usually tends to reject any employee proposal automatically. In the adversary environment of American organizations, to admit that employees have a good idea is to capitulate to them. To accept a proposal is to diminish one's authority, to lose face.

CASE #10
Bottom-up Installation

A group of production welders were upset about the time it took to process their recertification panels. As much as a month might pass between the time they welded the panels and the certification papers were delivered. After analyzing the situation in their quality circle, they determined that it resulted from three factors. First, the process involved five different departments in the plant—quality control, welding, machine shop, quality laboratories, and training. Second, shifting test panels between these shops involved no less than six separate moves, all of them requiring documentation and computer inputs as well as a forklift. Finally, no single individual, shop, or department had responsibility for the system. It just happened, and poorly.

To solve the problem, the welders proposed a new system in which all steps—cutting, milling, testing, and so on—would occur in one location under a single authority responsible for the entire process. Their major argument was presented to management with flow charts which showed that the new system would reduce the time it took to process the panels by four fifths.

Management (in this case, directors of manufacturing and quality with their relevant managers and general foremen) had attended a presentation on the quality circle process. But they had never been specifically trained in their roles. No one told them precisely how to receive a presentation from employees, how to arrive at a group decision, and how to follow through after the presentation.

When the pitch ended and discussion began, the managers sounded cautious. Though the argument was clear-cut and discussion indicated that they found the proposal feasible and even desirable, the production director, his manager of the welding and machine shops, and the foreman of the machine shop all seemed reluctant. They offered to "do a better job with the present system." They attacked the new proposal on the basis of cost, but the circle quickly showed that it was cost-effective. They next blamed the welders for not demanding that their supervisors insist on making the present system function. Although management did not defeat the proposal, these tactics succeeded in delaying the decision. The directors ordered the manager and his general foreman to review the proposal and get back to the circle with their plan to implement it.

A week passed, then a month, then two months, without a word. It was clear that they were intending to ignore the proposal. They had treated the presentation as a charade. To counter, the circle approached the two directors again and demanded an immediate response. The directors called the manager, and the manager called a meeting of the circle. In the meantime, he and his foreman developed an alternative plan. They would color-code panels so that their movement through the present system would be expedited. They even went ahead and implemented their plan in the hope that it would speed the procedure and the welders would forget about the problem.

When the meeting began, the general foreman spoke first. He outlined the color-code system, suggesting that it was the better solution because it would speed up panel processing without the need for a new system. Before he could finish, however, the manager interrupted him and began to ad lib. He fumbled about for a while, then came out and said that they planned to put the circle's proposal into effect immediately. It was the best solution, he said. The color-code system was just an interim measure.

No one knows why he changed his mind in the middle of the meeting. Perhaps the logic of the circle's proposal finally swayed him. Perhaps he recognized that it was good politics to accept their solution. For whatever reason, he announced that he would initiate a request to move the equipment into the laboratory.

Within a week the request was signed, but again the project showed signs of dying from neglect. Now the quality manager of the laboratory dragged his feet. Moreover, the circle soon learned that the general foreman of the machine shop lobbied daily with the manufacturing manager to stop the project. He did not want his tools moved, and, most of all, he did not want employees telling him to do so.

There matters stood for some time. The circle made repeated requests to the directors, insisting that they must keep their promises. Nothing happened. Some members lost interest and began to skip meetings, even though the circle was in the midst of another, more important, project. The message was clear. Right or wrong, any proposal represented a threat to management's self-proclaimed prerogative to make *all* decisions. Unless extensively prepared for quality circles, management would resist them.

After direct intervention by the quality circle office, the solution was implemented and the welding quality circle proceeded to another project. The whole process had taken more than a year.

• • •

The top-down strategy, on the other hand, errs on the side of caution. It repeatedly delays the formation of quality circles. The problem is that management's readiness for quality circles cannot be tested unless circles already exist. Lectures, seminars, demonstrations, and classroom exercises go just so far. In the end, managers have to learn about quality circles in context, by making real decisions and seeing the outcomes.

CASE #11
Top-down Installation

The organization development office of a large manufacturing firm on the East Coast received orders to investigate and implement quality circles. Preliminary studies indicated that a fully developed quality circle program would involve a 180-degree shift in management style. Management at the plant could be characterized as rigid, traditional, highly centralized, and autocratic. Managers viewed employees with suspicion, and after generations of an adversarial attitude, employees returned it. Moreover, management automatically challenged and evaluated new ideas, not on merit, but apparently on the personal or political strength of the proponent. Superiors tended to have an attitude toward their subordinates that could be summarized as "Don't bother me with 'buts,' just do it!" They prided themselves on their toughness.

The organization development office decided that it had to change management's style before it could install quality circles, and so planned and organized a series of presentations by outside speakers. Consultants lectured. Quality circle program administrators from other organizations presented videotapes of successful circles in action. When the opportunity arose, the organization development office persuaded the plant manager, as well as some of his directors, to attend a two-day seminar on participative management. It sent lower managers to other seminars. After each of these events, managers remarked on the importance of what they had heard, and said they understood its significance. But inevitably, back in the day-to-day routine, they continued to operate as always. Nothing changed.

All this took nearly a year. But having committed itself to changing management before implementing circles, the organization development office persisted in its plan and decided to determine management's readiness to accept quality circles with an attitude questionnaire. This took time to develop and so another year passed without one circle having been formed.

Combining Strategies: Middle-down

To avoid the problems and pitfalls of both top-down and bottom-up strategies and still retain their advantages, you should follow the following three-step strategy that combines the two.

First, when *selling* the idea of quality circles, proceed from the top down. Direct your presentations first to executive management and the union, then to middle management, and, finally, to employees.

Second, when *installing* quality circles, use a middle-down strategy. First, train middle managers (from manager through foreman in Diagram 1) so that they understand the objectives of the program, their role in it, and its benefits for them. Next, train first-line supervisors as quality circle leaders. Finally, train members in group problem solving and group decision making.

Third, begin with a *pilot program* to practice the art of advising quality circles and to learn how to do it. Proceed slowly and deliberately, department by department, through the entire organization.

Experience, rather than theory, fostered this approach, which overcomes the greatest single obstacle to successful installation of quality circles: resistance by middle managers. It also avoids two major contributors to that problem: moving too fast and failing to include a supervisor in each circle.

Resistance by middle management. Middle managers resist quality circles for a number of reasons: they have not been included in the installation strategy, they lack comprehension of the benefits of the quality circle process and lack understanding of their role in the quality circle process, and they fear that the process will give employees access to upper management.

Failure to include middle managers in an installation strategy is common. Typically, executive management decides that it wants quality circles and designates an office to design a program and implement it. The office, with more enthusiasm than experience, begins immediately to recruit employees. The employees respond with excitement and quickly identify problems, develop solutions, and present them formally. Executive management is pleased and approves the proposals. Employees are delighted. However, the entire process, from the beginning of the program through the management presentation, excludes middle management. Not surprisingly, middle managers feel little desire to support quality circles or their projects.

Even after formal presentations, most middle managers misinterpret the purpose of the quality circle process and its benefits. This frustrates many administrators, trainers, and advisors but, in truth, there is little in the experience of most middle managers to prepare them to understand quality circles—and much to mislead them. For years, social scientists and management consultants have told them, in books, seminars, and training films, to respond to their employees, pay more attention to employees' "personal needs," improve the "human relations" in their work group, upgrade the "quality of work life," "listen more and talk less," and "maximize the potential" of every employee. Too often, however, this advice has been offered without describing the practical means—the actual machinery—with which such ideas might be put to work. To middle managers, these humanistic directives often seemed naive, if not disruptive, when matched against real work as they knew it—production deadlines, machinery breakdowns, regulations, procedures, and employee incompetence and hostility. Thus, without extensive indoctrination into the actual workings of the quality circle process, and without statistical demonstrations of its effect on employees, middle managers may, with some justification, confuse quality circles with previous reform efforts. To them, it is just another do-gooder's attempt to meddle in their business.

Though they usually deny it, middle managers fear quality circles because they give employees access to upper management. Middle managers can and do rule absolutely by monopolizing the flow of information between upper management and employees. They prefer to tell upper management only good news; if the news is bad, they tell as little as they can get away with. In turn, they tell employees only those things, and in the proper slant, that serve their needs. Any additional channel, any competition to their monopoly, directly threatens their authority.

CASE #12
The Middle Manager Turnaround

When the production welders described in Case #10 finished preparing recommendations for welder recertification panels, they made a series of presentations to middle management before going to upper management. They presented it to their general foreman, Bricker, a man they knew well and whose opinion they valued. Bricker listened attentively to their pitch and in an informal feedback session offered advice to strengthen their argument. When asked if he agreed with the proposal, Bricker said that it would be a definite improvement, and he hoped that upper management would accept it. In a second session, the circle presented the proposal to engineers and various support people who had helped develop it. Bricker attended and again expressed approval of the idea and his support for it. There was no indication that he had any reservations at all.

When the group made its formal presentation to management, which included the general foreman's manager and director and the director of quality control, Bricker did an about-face. He made it look as though the circle had blown the problem way out of proportion, and he resented the implication that he had not been doing his job, an opinion never expressed in the previous sessions. Bricker concluded that the whole matter could be cleared up by a single change in the present system. There was no need for the elaborate solution proposed by the circle.

Circle members, especially the supervisor-leader, were shocked. Although they eventually won agreement for their proposal, they felt betrayed by Bricker. They discussed it at length in their regular meeting the following week and concluded that he had simply wilted in the face of criticism from upper management.

There was more to it than that. By a simple act of omission—by not reporting problems—Bricker had communicated to upper management that he had everything in his area under control. In previous sessions, with upper management absent, he could agree with the circle members that the problem existed. They knew it and he knew it. But suddenly, in the presence of his management, his employees advertised the problem and made Bricker look incompetent, or so he felt. He was trapped in a predicament of his own making. He could no longer send two messages—one for management and one for employees. Bricker had to choose, and he took the predictable course. He maintained he assured tone of his earlier message to management: "No problems down here."

• • •

A middle-down strategy goes a long way toward solving the problem of middle management resistance. Of course, it cannot resolve the trauma of giving employees access to all levels of management. That access is an inherent part of the quality circle process, and middle managers have to learn to deal with it. The middle-down strategy does, however, give them a greater sense of ownership of quality circles by training them first and allowing them to sponsor the training of their subordinates. They control, at least partially, the installation process. It also provides them with an in-depth understanding of the quality circle process and their role within it, and thus alleviates some of their fears.

Moving too fast. Moving too quickly in installing quality circles defeats even the best intentions. The cause is simple naivete. Program administrators who see the benefits but lack appreciation of both the subtle and obvious difficulties rush to form as many circles as possible in the shortest amount of time. Presumably, they reason that more is better. It's an American disease.

CASE #13
The Sorcerer's Apprentice

In a large southwestern electronics firm, a program administrator obtained training materials and began forming circles single-handedly. It seemed easy. The environment was right and the need was there. Various shops responded quickly. The administrator, Russell, followed the basic premise: give employees the time and tools to put their ideas to work and the details will take care of themselves.

Rather than obtain additional help, Russell chose to train and advise the circles himself. Using prepared slides and manuals, he had little difficulty developing a training course. He simply turned on the machine and handed out the books. Within a year he had more than thirty circles going. Each required some degree of guidance and support, things that could be provided only by attending their meetings, but Russell had a lot of energy. He came in early and spent most of his day rushing from meeting to meeting.

After their first projects, some of the circles began to branch out. Rather than work on time-saving tools or various quality improvement techniques, they focused on more personal needs. One began to investigate an adjustment of certain job classification inequities that had annoyed its members for years. Another sought to meet more than one hour a week—the established and agreed-upon maximum. A third and fourth group simply stopped meeting, one bored with the whole thing and the other frustrated by the inability of the members to agree on anything.

The situation grew worse when a number of circles found they could not obtain essential technical support. One circle thought that they might be able to cut in half the time involved in their work process, but needed technical support from the engineering and industrial engineering departments to develop the idea. Although they had invited representatives of both groups to their meetings, neither department had bothered to send anyone. They were unaccustomed to working with quality circles.

The most serious problem, however, arose after a number of circles gave their first presentations. Their ideas were well received, and a few of the managers were tremendously impressed by the innovativeness of employees whom they had regarded as uncreative. They promised prompt action and seemed to do so in good faith. But six months later, little or nothing had been done, and the ideas had been preempted by "more important matters."

In the face of these difficulties, Russell began to grumble about management sabotage and lack of management support. He finally resigned, finding a position in another department. The quality circle effort went out of control.

• • •

A pilot program of four or five circles over a year's time allows you to avoid these problems. It gives you the opportunity to identify difficulties and develop solutions before the sheer volume of those difficulties overwhelms the office. It allows time to absorb the reactions and gain the confidence of your organization. At the same time, a pilot program gives the organization an opportunity to adjust to the existence of quality circles and to learn to appreciate their usefulness without feeling inundated.

Excluding the supervisor. Many people think that quality circles should not include a supervisor, believing that employees will be more open and productive without that inhibiting presence. This is true, but leaving the supervisor out of the circle—either by design or by his or her reluctance to participate—creates a number of additional problems that far outweigh the added openness gained by the supervisor's absence.

To begin with, a seldom stated but important goal of quality circles is to strengthen the ties between employees and their supervisors, or, at the very least, not to worsen them. If the supervisor is excluded, the quality circle process can undermine this goal. If the supervisor has no sense of ownership, any conflict with employees may be exacerbated rather than lessened. The conflict can be over something as simple as the circle's standard meeting time and the supervisor's production schedule. If the meeting must be postponed because of a production schedule, the employees may feel that the supervisor is sabotaging their circle. Such a postponement creates no ill will, however, if the supervisor is as much involved with the circle as the employees.

A supervisor will feel threatened when excluded from the circle process. Not only is there a loss of control over employees for one hour each week, but problems may be exposed to upper management which result in some embarrassment for the supervisor, as in the example of the general foreman in Case #12. This potential threat can be blown out of all proportion, particularly if the employees choose to exploit the supervisor's fear and use it to torment him and undermine his authority. That is what happened in Case #3, where the tool fabricators made the *supervisors* the problem. However, to use an old cliché, if the supervisor is *in* the circle, the threat disappears and he becomes part of the solution.

Most important, without a supervisor in the circle, in-line management cannot feel that it owns its quality circles. The normal chain of command is broken. Middle managers have no sure way of knowing what is going on in a circle—if it is doing well, if it is stumbling, or if it is doing nothing. As a result, they cease to think of it as their circle and their responsibility.

When this happens, ownership of a circle reverts to the quality circle office. Middle managers assume that the advisor runs the circle meetings and they hold the quality circle office responsible for the success or failure of the circle. At the same time, the circle members begin to act toward the advisor and quality circle office as they would to another command structure. They turn to it for help in righting the injustices and inequities of the official management structure. If they are motivated to try, they may even attempt to use it to circumvent and, thus, undermine the official structure, again as in Case #3.

In this situation, when the advisor tries to control a circle, its members transfer all their hostility toward their official supervisor to the new, unofficial supervisor—the advisor. Eventually the advisor loses any ability to influence the circle. In the end, the circle veers out of control, antagonistic toward everyone and frustrated in its attempts to solve problems.

At the other extreme, the absence of a supervisor can cause members to lose interest and disband their circle. (See Diagram 6.) On the one hand, they may feel insecure and incapable of succeeding without the supervisor's guidance. On the other, they may feel that his absence expresses a lack of interest on the part of management, so they give up before even beginning, not wanting to be humiliated by losing a presentation. In short, a supervisor is both the natural leader of the work group and a symbol of management support for the quality circle effort. Either way, his absence undermines the circle.

This raises the question of leadership. Should the supervisor serve as circle leader? From the point of view of the middle-down strategy, the answer is clear. He should be the leader and every effort must be made to support him in his role. He must be trained in the quality circle concept and process, and must also receive the best possible instruction in the role of quality circle leader. Part of the responsibility of a circle leader is to train the other members; thus the leader should receive instruction in training employees in the techniques of group problem solving.

Unfortunately, like middle managers, many supervisors often resist participating in quality circles. The rea-

DIAGRAM 6

Quality circle without a supervisor/leader.

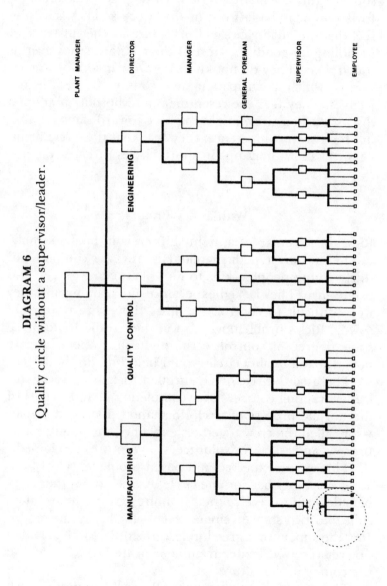

sons for this are many. In poorly designed installation efforts they may be left out of the process. They may also feel that the quality circle effort is just another instance of meddling do-goodism. Most of the resistance, however, is due to fear. They do not know how to run an open meeting in which participation and consensus are the objectives. They fear the resentment and hostility that open discussion in a circle might provoke toward them. Doubting their own competence, they fear that the circle members will show them up. In short, circles threaten them.

CASE #14
With and Without

Rick, the foreman of a night-shift crew in final assembly, wanted to start a quality circle. His crew was composed of thirty young people—kids to him—between eighteen and twenty-five. They lacked experience and training and they were difficult to control. At times they were downright rowdy. Rick's problem was to win their respect and bring some degree of control to the night-shift operation. He hoped that a quality circle would help him do this.

The quality circle office enrolled Rick in a supervisor-leader training course. After completing it, and as part of the normal process of circle formation, Rick and his advisor called the crew together, explained the quality circle process, and asked for volunteers. The entire crew joined.

This was unexpected and posed problems. Thirty was too large a number for one circle. As a solution, the members decided to receive their training as a group and then split into two smaller circles, each with fifteen members. Jim, the supervisor, agreed to lead the other circle. He had not yet received leader training, but he hoped to attend the course in the future.

The two circles started off well enough. Each brainstormed a list of items that were plaguing them all.

They agreed to choose different problems as their first projects. It slowly became apparent, however, that Rick's group was doing considerably better than Jim's. In Rick's circle, the members openly listed supervision as a problem, discussed it directly with Rick, and then, having discharged their frustrations, slowly began to isolate a problem that they could solve quickly.

At first, Rick moderated each discussion, acting as a catalyst as he listed items on the blackboard. By the third and fourth sessions, however, he delegated these tasks from time to time and assumed the role of ordinary member. By session five, the circle had focused on the problem of training, or lack of it, for workers on the second shift. Within a few more sessions, they had listed the types of training they needed and made a case for its importance. They presented their list to the director of training on the night shift. They even proposed that he devise a course to teach them how to teach their fellow workers on the job. He did so, and the members quickly shared their growing expertise. More important, however, was the fact that Rick had succeeded in winning undisputed leadership of his crew by tying his needs to those of his employees in a single project.

Jim's group, in contrast, could not reach agreement on the problem they wanted to tackle. In fact, they never did. Their difficulties related to leadership. Whether from lack of training or lack of talent, Jim could not relax in the circle setting. He appeared to feel inadequate as a leader of circle activities, but at the same time he was unable to relinquish leadership, probably out of fear that he would not then be able to control the situation. He shifted from dictating what the members would choose as a project, to claiming in defense of the *status quo* that there were no problems, to retiring from the discussion altogether, appearing confused about what to do next. Frustrated, he began to miss meetings. When the advisor spoke to him about his poor attendance, Jim ridiculed the members, claiming that they were incapable of serious work. Eventually he resigned from the circle with the excuse that he was having "personal problems at home."

Unfortunately, no one in the circle surfaced as a leader to replace him. Various members volunteered to moderate discussion and lead the meetings, but none seemed to command the respect of the group. They accomplished little except when the advisor joined them and led their discussions. Interest dwindled and, over a four-month period, membership declined to four or five stalwarts who spent most of their time complaining that management had abandoned them. Finally, recognizing the stunning success of the other circle, the remaining four voted to abolish their circle and join the first.

• • •

A middle-down strategy in which supervisors receive extensive training—training in the quality circle process, for their role as circle members and circle leaders, and, especially, for their role as one of the trainers of the other members—goes a long way toward overcoming all the problems that can arise in an installation program. Indeed, in many ways the well-planned involvement of well-trained supervisors is the key to success. The organization, through the supervisor, demonstrates its commitment to the quality circle process. Only through the supervisor can the quality circle process ever truly become part of the normal management process.

Full-time Versus Part-time Advisors

Advisors for promoting, supporting, and evaluating quality circles may be assigned on a full-time basis or part-time. Each approach has distinct advantages and disadvantages.

Before deciding which to follow, you should, as program administrator, carefully evaluate the pros and cons of each approach against the needs of your organization and its probable response to quality circles.

Full-time advisors: Full-time advisors work exclusively for a quality circle program administrator. They promote, support, monitor, and measure quality circles. In many instances they also assume the role of trainer. In short, their personal careers relate directly to the well-being of the quality circle effort and, particularly, the circles with which they work.

There are two major advantages to having a staff of full-time advisors. First, they provide the professional expertise necessary to implement all facets of an installation program, and, second, they provide the control needed to keep managers and employees from distorting the quality circle process before it is fully understood. In one installation program with which I am familiar, there are four full-time advisors. In addition to attending every circle meeting and advising the leaders and members, the advisors also train managers, leaders, and members. Furthermore, each has a specialized responsibility. One develops and updates training materials. Another designed an attitude questionnaire which he asks all circle members to fill out on a regular basis. A third maintains a system for collecting and analyzing data about the impact of quality circles on the output of the organization (for example, such things as defect rates and employee turnover). The fourth maintains a file of successful quality circle presentations and issues a handbook of successful projects twice a year.

With this centralized and specialized staff, the program administrator can monitor the day-to-day activities of every circle and circle leader. He or she can also closely watch the impact of the quality circle effort on the organization. The program administrator can, through this staff of advisors, identify and respond to the many crises that arise in the early stages of an implementation effort. And when a crisis is resolved and a lesson is learned, a centralized staff of advisors, each working with ten or twenty circles, can retain, share, and communicate the lesson rapidly. Finally, the advisory staff can enable the program administrator to maintain a standardized set of rules and procedures and see to it that they are followed.

The disadvantages of full-time advisors appear only after the program has operated for some time. The concentration of full-time advisors in one office, separate from the rest of the organization, reinforces the view that ownership of the quality circle effort lies with the quality circle office and not the organization as a whole. It certainly seems that way to managers. In addition, creating full-time advisors tends to institutionalize the advisor role rather than the circle process. Despite training courses for managers, leaders, and members, most people do not understand the role of advisor. They press, consciously or unconsciously, for advisors to function as leaders. They assume that advisors are responsible for the success or failure of the circles they work with. Finally, most full-time advisors feel uncomfortable to some extent in a new and ill-defined role. They sense that managers and employees do not recognize the advisor's function as a valued job. It is not "real" work. To compensate, advisors may take on tasks that make them indispensable to the success of the quality circle and the quality circle effort, and this undermines the objective of incorporating the quality circle process into the normal management process.

CASE #15
The Overzealous Advisor

Frank was determined to succeed as an advisor. He attended every meeting of the circles assigned to him, he met with leaders before and after each circle meeting, he contacted members outside of meetings to keep up with their feelings about their circle's progress. He tracked down and interviewed any member who failed to attend a session. He visited work areas to be sure he understood the problems discussed by circle members.

In circle meetings, he offered his opinions freely and openly. When the opportunity arose, he intervened with mini-lectures on problem-solving techniques that might help the circle. He raised issues that he felt circle members missed. He questioned circle actions and asked dumb questions or played devil's advocate. He acted as a cheerleader, and from time to time he even got mad. Frank did everything he thought might help the members solve their problem as a group.

As time passed, he became more skilled. He learned to guide the behavior of circle members without their awareness. He could elicit responses from members simply by gazing inquisitively at them. He could measure the pace of discussion and at the right moment marshal consensus on an issue.

Frank knew the danger of this role. He knew that he must use his skills to support the leader and to promote participation by all the members. He was convinced that he handled the problem with care, but despite his awareness, certain leaders in his circles began to feel inadequate and suggested that they would resign. None did, but a few of them never seemed to have the time to attend meetings. In their absence, Frank took on the role of leader. He felt, and perhaps he was right, that extraordinary circumstances called for direct intervention. He could worry later about building strong leadership. After all, a weak circle was always better than no circle at all. And he could not afford to "lose a circle."

Frank found himself fulfilling another role. When circles requested it, he made their audio and visual aids for them. When they needed it, he contacted engineers and other support specialists. When circles made presentations, he arranged for the room and put out the memo inviting the appropriate managers. After presentations, he called engineering or finance to make sure that they implemented the proposals.

As time went on, Frank found himself very much in demand. With fifteen circles to advise, he had a minimum of fifteen hours of meetings each week, and for each hour spent in a circle meeting another hour was spent in preparation. After each meeting, he took thirty minutes to write a report on the circle's progress. He also trained managers and new circle leaders, and when a project was accepted, he worked with the relevant managers and support people to make sure that it was implemented. He was content and found his job full and rewarding.

At the end of two years, Frank experienced a complete turnaround. He felt tired and frustrated, racing day after day to keep up with twenty-five circles. He felt like a secretary, a "go-fer." Visual aids, meeting arrangements, and meeting notes were all he had time for—just barely. Worse still, circle leaders kept failing him. They should run meetings, see to arrangements for presentations, and make contacts with support people, yet they always seemed to need help. He found himself "leading" half of his circles. Two had even folded.

Perhaps most frustrating of all was the fact that many managers, even those in departments with the most impressive results, did not regard quality circles as an important activity. They complained that the circles robbed them of one hour each week per crew, and saw them as disruptive, despite statistics which showed overwhelming improvement in employee attitudes. Even in the face of hard statistics on reductions in defects and safety incidents for their areas, they did not seem to pay any more than lip service to the concept. On top of this, when a circle encountered difficulty, the managers called Frank to straighten it out.

After two years and three months, Frank quit quality circles and transferred to the personnel department. When he left, five more of "his" circles folded.

• • •

What happened to Frank can happen to any advisor. Unwittingly, he began to compete with the designated leader of the circle and eventually found himself victorious. At the same time, and as part of the same quiet struggle for power, Frank took over all interactions between the circle and the organization. He became a middleman, a broker. He, not the circle leader or the circle members, controlled interaction and communication with the organization. Diagram 7 shows how that happens.

This kind of brokering by an advisor can result in an overdependency on the quality circle office. If carried too far, it leaves the quality circles directly dependent on the advisor and indirectly on the office. And if the advisor leaves or if the office is shut down, the circles may die. In short, a staff of full-time advisors carries with it the danger of institutionalizing the quality circle office and the advisor role rather than the quality circle process. In an extreme situation, the office may even begin to function as a separate hierarchy that challenges and subverts the normal chain of command. This is a particularly easy trap to fall into if relations between employees and the organization are traditionally antagonistic. If employees dislike their supervisor, the advisor, eager to gain their respect, may allow employees to use him or her as a channel to bypass the supervisor.

Finally, there is the problem of empire building. A single advisor can work with a maximum of about fifteen

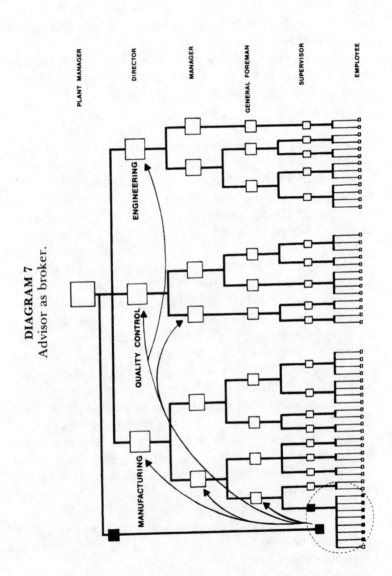

DIAGRAM 7
Advisor as broker.

circles. Therefore, as the number of circles grows, the office must grow—one advisor for each fifteen circles. Theoretically, each circle should eventually stand on its own, with only occasional assistance from an advisor. In practice, however, this is not always easy to achieve. In theory, a program administrator should always strive to institutionalize quality circles within the normal management process and thus reduce the function of his office to training and simple maintenance. However, the inherent forces of the organization can push the program administrator into demonstrating the office's importance by expanding and hiring more advisors—by building an empire. Diagram 8 depicts the effects.

These problems are not insurmountable. They are only *possible* dangers. They can be avoided by dedicated program administrators and advisors who resist the temptations to lead circles, to broker relations between circles and the organization, and to build bureaucratic empires. It simply takes people-wise and organization-wise individuals who have the training and experience to understand the idea that they must work themselves out of a job.

Part-time advisors: Part-time advisors do not work directly for the program administrator. They are volunteers who have regular, full-time jobs in the organization—as engineers, supervisors, mechanics, buyers, typists, keypunchers, managers—and work only part-time as advisors, usually with only one circle. They support, advise, and monitor their circle, but do not, as a rule, train circle members or measure the results of circle participation.

The advantages of part-time advisors contrast with those of full-time advisors. Rather than concentrating ownership in one office, they spread it around the organization. Usually, the part-time advisor of a circle in one department works for a circle in an entirely different department, creating a web of interrelationships. (See Dia-

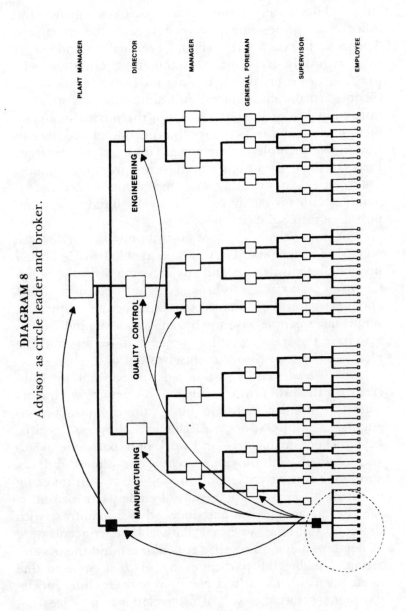

DIAGRAM 8
Advisor as circle leader and broker.

gram 9.) This approach reduces the chance of advisors coopting leadership and brokering circle activities. Since part-time advisors work with only one circle, and their circle work is not their sole activity—or even a major source of their organizational identity and income—they are less pressed to become circle leaders or middlemen between the circle and the organization. Drawing part-time advisors from a department without quality circles helps to seed the idea before actually forming circles. Finally, part-time advisors remove the danger of empire buildings. They are only voluntary, part-time employees of the program administrator and are officially responsible to other people in the organization.

The disadvantages of part-time advisors also contrast with those of full-time advisors. Because they are volunteers, part-time advisors must receive training prior to working with a circle. This necessitates an additional training course, with the ensuing costs in time and materials. Though part-time advisors report to the quality circle office and thus provide a limited amount of control over the installation program, they offer considerably less control than full-time advisors. Because they are only part-time, they quickly abandon their circles when the workloads of their regular jobs become heavy. Finally, and most important, having many part-time advisors makes it difficult for the program administrator to standardize rules and procedures and maintain them, because efforts to modify and distort the quality circle process may be numerous and might conflict.

It should be pointed out that part-time advisors do not offer much of an advantage in cost. To operate an installation program with part-time advisors, you still need a permanent staff of trainers to lead courses for managers, leaders, members, and advisors. Moreover, a part-time advisor costs the organization one hour per week in meeting

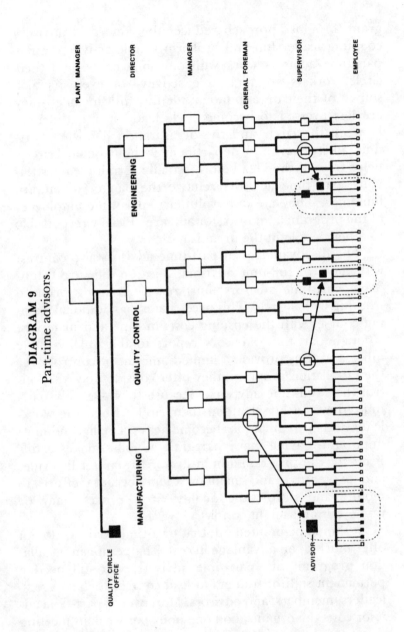

DIAGRAM 9
Part-time advisors.

time, plus one hour in preparation and follow-up. At this rate, the cost of fifteen part-time advisors can easily equal, perhaps even surpass, the cost of one full-time advisor for the same number of circles. In the end, the choice between part-time and full-time advisors is a matter of *how* to spend the money, not *how much* to spend.

At the present stage of development of quality circles in the United States, it is impossible to say which approach works best. Each seems to have an appropriate place depending on the specific organizational environment. Base your choice on an understanding of the management style of your organization. If your organization has a tradition of authoritarian management, coupled with strong resistance from middle management and supervision, the full-time advisor is probably the more appropriate choice. If your organization has a more flexible and innovative management, and especially if it is a new organization, the part-time advisor might be best. You might also consider a mixed system—a cadre of full-time advisors plus part-time advisors in various departments.

Whichever approach is taken, keep in mind the long-term objective of quality circle installation. You want to hand the quality circle process—slowly—over to the organization. Middle managers and supervisors will someday carry out most of the major functions: promoting, forming, advising, and following up on projects. In this light, the full-time-advisor approach buys survival of the quality circle effort in a hostile environment in the early stages, at a cost of difficulty in handing over the functions to the organization later on. In contrast, the part-time approach buys ease in transferring the functions, but at the cost of weakened centralized control. The emphasis on part-time advisors assumes strong organizational support, while the full-time-advisor approach assumes stronger organizational resistance.

Some might argue that it would be less expensive and would more directly serve the interests of building the quality circle process into normal management practice to do away with the advisor and let the supervisor promote and run the circle himself. Not so. As a regular participant in circle meetings, the advisor serves three essential functions. First, he sees to it that the members put their training to work and that they receive the "in-the-circle" instruction necessary for successfully solving problems. Second, he monitors the activities of a circle to make sure that the members adhere to the rules of the quality circle process and do not distort its intent. And third, perhaps his most important function is to ensure that the supervisor does not dominate and smother the circle. In one sense, he acts as a referee, ready to step in if the supervisor attempts to direct the group in a traditional, authoritarian manner. On the other hand, he acts as a counterweight, another leader who, in structural terms, presents an alternative authority and thus prevents a supervisor from monopolizing the group.

Taking the Final Step

Choosing advisors, whether full-time or part-time, is only the first step. As we have seen in the Toyota Auto Body case, the second and final step must involve transferring the responsibility for training and advising from the quality circle office to the staffs of the major departments of the organization. The office retains the responsibility only for producing materials and, perhaps, measuring results.

To achieve this goal, you must eventually place an advisor as consultant to each major department at the level of manager or director, as shown in Diagram 10. From this position as consultant, he will advise managers, general

DIAGRAM 10
Decentralized quality circle office staff with advisors
in each major department.

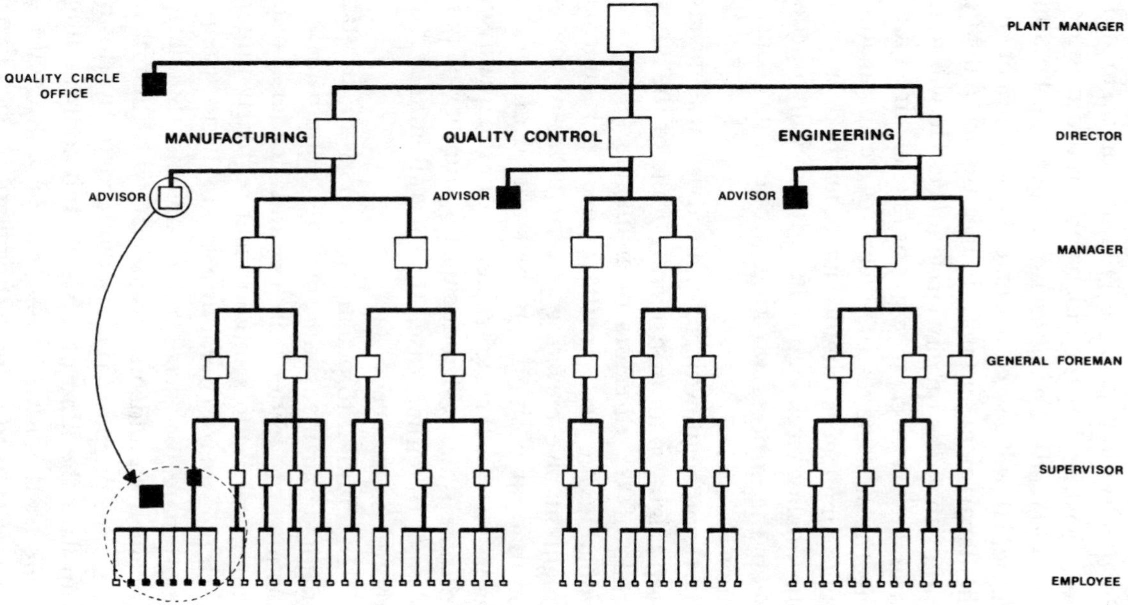

foremen, and supervisors in their roles as participants in the quality circle process. He will train them and the members, ensure that the rules and procedures are followed, and intercede if a supervisor appears to be dominating a circle. He will also coordinate the activities of circles within the department and may, in fact, report to the department rather than the quality circle office. He will not, however, attend every circle meeting or take as direct a role as during the first stages of quality circle installation. By this stage, managers should have learned how to operate the quality circles and the advisor will function only to keep the process working properly by consulting with them.

If you begin with full-time advisors, achieving this final step might entail transferring some of the advisors to the staffs of key directors or managers and eventually terminating the rest. In the case of part-time advisors, it might involve elevating one or more of the advisors to permanent positions on the staffs of directors and managers or transferring trainers from the quality circle office to these staffs and reducing the number of part-time advisors. In either case, the overall number of advisors should be reduced.

In addition to placing advisors with the staffs of each major department, the final step should include the formation of leader circles and leader councils. The supervisor-leaders should meet regularly under the leadership of their general foreman to discuss their circles and coordinate projects and problems. Similarly, general foremen should meet regularly with their managers for the same purpose. If carried out correctly, this process will supplant the kind of advising and coordinating formerly done by the advisors and will permit a reduction in the advisor staff to a single consultant in each department.

Summary

You should adopt a strategy in which you first inform the entire organization of the quality circle concept and its objectives and then begin installation, on a pilot basis, by training middle managers first, supervisors second, and employees third. This sequence overcomes the inherent resistance of middle management to quality circles. It also overcomes problems that arise from rapid installation which fails to involve supervisors as leaders. Within this strategy, the choice between full-time and part-time advisors depends on the program administrator's evaluation of the organization. In an organization with a tradition of extreme authoritarian leadership and a history of conflict between employees and management, the full-time approach is appropriate. In an organization that already has a participative management style, part-time advisors are preferable. In either case, plan for the office to retain only the tasks of providing materials and measuring results and to eventually turn over the training and advisory functions to in-line management by placing advisors within, and making them answerable to, each department. Finally, form leader circles and leader councils to ensure direct involvement and ownership by middle managers.

6
Training

Over the course of time, patterns of behavior in an organization become traditional. But the quality circle requires particular behavior that may conflict with the traditional patterns, and therefore people need formal training in how to fill their new roles—training in what to say and do, and when and how. Without it, circle members and leaders, as well as managers, may fail. Installing quality circles without adequate training is like asking people to put on a play without revealing plot, roles, or lines to the actors.

CASE #16
The Agenda

A group of mechanical assemblers met for nearly six months as a quality circle. They had received training in various participative problem-solving techniques, such as cause-and-effect diagrams, flow charts, and brainstorming. But because of the newness of the quality circle effort, they lacked experience and the basic skills for running a meeting. As a result, they floundered.

The original supervisor-leader was transferred after two months, and his replacement was so overworked that he did not attend meetings. In his place, the circle secretary, who was also the lead man of the work crew, presided. He did the best he could, but every meeting seemed to wander aimlessly with a great deal of discussion and little resolution. Members grumbled that they accomplished nothing. Some, skeptical of the entire process, stopped attending. Slowly, meetings became joke sessions, dominated by more mischievious members.

The group's advisor worried that the circle would fold. He discussed the matter with other advisors of more experience and discovered there had been insufficient preparation and training of the participants.

He immediately prepared a written outline of an agenda, including all the abstract steps that each meeting should contain—opening the meeting, taking attendance, reading the minutes, reporting pending action items, discussing action items, discussing new business, assigning new action items, preparing for the next meeting, summarizing and closing the meeting. He distributed copies to the mechanics and discussed it with them, insisting that they keep a copy in the circle manual and refer to it before each meeting.

The effect was instantaneous. The group followed the agenda conscientiously, referring to it repeatedly throughout each meeting to make sure that every step was fulfilled. Within a month the group cleared up a number of minor problems in their work area and began to tackle one large, difficult problem. Membership not only steadied, it began to increase as the skeptics returned.

• • •

Good training programs provide participants with clear descriptions of the roles they must play in the quality circle process and the techniques they must employ to succeed in these roles. For example, members, leader, and advisor must learn their basic roles for a circle meeting. They must also learn problem solving, leadership, and advisory techniques that will help them perform successfully. For management presentations, members and leader must literally rehearse their parts as if performing a play, with the advisor serving as stage director. In the same context, managers and technical specialists feel more comfortable if they are taught how to react—how to play the role of audience. They must also learn to fulfill their role as authorities who implement the circle's proposal.

Trainers should employ two equally important approaches in teaching these roles. On the one hand, they should describe the roles verbally and visually—a cognitive approach. On the other hand, they should rehearse participants in their roles—a behavioral approach. Every course, indeed every session, should contain equal parts of both approaches, closely integrated, since most employees will resist traditional classroom lectures.

For example, participants should have their role in a given context defined for them through lectures, viewgraphs, written rules and case studies, videotapes, and slides or movies. Then they should rehearse the role with exercises, games, or full-dress presentations. The order may be reversed, with participants acting out a role first and then defining it through group discussion.

A quality circle training program addresses four major roles: circle member, circle leader, manager-technical specialist, and advisor. A specifically designed course should be given for each of these roles at intervals appropriate to the installation schedule. Ideally, you should prepare the courses prior to forming your first circle and apply them in the sequence outlined in the previous chapter—train advisors, managers, and technical specialists first, then supervisors who will lead the circles, and finally, have the advisors and supervisors train the circle members.

Because they focus on individuals who come from different work areas and who will work with different circles, training courses for advisors, leaders, managers, and technical specialists can be held regularly, with participants attending whenever their individual schedules permit. The training course for members, however, focuses on employees who regularly work together and who will form a problem-solving *group,* a quality circle. Its objective, then, involves more than teaching a new role. It also welds the members together into a functioning group under one leader. With this in mind, it is preferable to train the members as a group simultaneously.

This objective of simultaneous training for all circle members may be difficult to achieve, because not all employees volunteer at once. Some join only after they see their companions enjoying the experience. To get late joiners and newly hired employees "up to speed," you have two alternatives. Either you can schedule a course for circle members that just teaches the basics and does not attempt to form a group, or you can reduce the content of the member course to videotape or slides, plus exercises in a manual. The choice depends, of course, on time, money, equipment, and personnel.

Outlining Courses

This chapter does not present specific materials for the four basic training courses needed to implement quality circles. To do so would require three or four manuals, far more space than this format allows. Moreover, very good training materials can be purchased from consultants or through the International Association of Quality Circles. Or, if you wish, you can write your own materials based on those already published.

With this in mind, I present only the objectives—which

are the same for all categories of trainee—and an outline of issues and topics that each course should cover. These objectives and outlines can serve as a "shopping list" to help evaluate materials and courses now available, or as guides for writing your own materials.

Objectives

A. Acquaint participants with the quality circle process and its benefits for them and for the organization.
B. Allay any fears or doubts they might have about quality circles.
C. Convince them to volunteer.
D. Prepare them to fulfill their role as members of a quality circle.
E. Acquaint them with the techniques of group problem solving.
F. Encourage them to feel that they own the circle and are responsible for it.

Course Outline for Training Members (employees)
Minimum Training Time: 10 hours, either once each week in the regular meeting or in a one-day, off-site session.
Taught by Advisor and Leader (Supervisor)

1. Motivating opener (for example, a videotape of the NBC white paper "If Japan Can, Why Can't We?").
2. Quality circle concept: structure and process.
3. Brief history of the development and spread of quality circles.
4. Basic meeting skills:
   a. Role of leader, members, secretary, and advisor
   b. Agenda
5. Basic quality circle problem-solving techniques:

a. Brainstorming
b. Flow charts
c. Pareto analysis *
d. Cause-and-effect diagrams
e. Histograms
f. Graphs
g. Control charts
h. Check sheets
i. Decision matrices
j. Cost-benefit analysis
6. Basic quality circle problem-solving process:
   a. Identifying a problem
   b. Analyzing the problem
   c. Generating solutions
   d. Choosing a solution
   e. Presenting the solution to management
   f. Implementing the solution
   g. Evaluating the solution
7. Rules of the quality circle process in your organization.

Course Outline for Training Leader (Supervisor)
Minimum Training Time: 16 hours, in a two-day, off-site session if possible. Taught by Trainer.

1. through 7. Same as for employee training.
8. Why some supervisors fear quality circles.
9. How quality circles can benefit the supervisor.
10. Participative versus authoritative leadership.
11. Planning, leading, and evaluating a quality circle meeting.

---

* A simple column graph in which the columns are arranged in descending order, from largest on left to smallest on right. Named after Vilfredo Pareto (1848–1923), Italian economist and sociologist.

12. The don'ts—what not to do as a circle leader.
13. Preparation to teach member course.

Course Outline for Training Manager and Technical Specialist

Minimum Training Time: 10 hours, in one-day, off-site session if possible. Taught by Trainer.

1. through 3. Same as for employee training.
4. Why some managers and technical specialists fear quality circles.
5. How quality circles can benefit managers and technical specialists.
6. How managers and technical specialists can support quality circles on a day-to-day basis.
7. Basic meeting skills (brief outline).
8. Basic quality circle problem-solving techniques (brief outline).
9. How to follow up on a quality circle proposal.
10. The don'ts—what not to do with quality circles.
11. Rules of the quality circle process in your organization.

Course Outline for Training Full-time or Part-time Advisor

Minimum training Time: 32 hours, in a four-day, off-site session if possible. Taught by Trainer.

1. through 7. Same as for employee training.
8. Why some managers, technical specialists, and supervisors fear quality circles.
9. How quality circles can benefit them.
10. Participative versus authoritative leadership.
11. Planning, leading, and evaluating a quality circle meeting.

12. Supporting the circle leader.
13. Advising the circle.
14. Dealing with managers and technical specialists.
15. Directing the preparations of a management presentation.
16. Reporting circle activities to the program administrator.
17. Following up circle proposals.
18. Evaluating circle progress and growth.
19. The don'ts—what not to do as an advisor.

Courses of this type seem to be so complex and difficult to develop that some organizations attempt to install quality circles without a training program. Training is important, however, and considering that the commitment to qualiy circles is a commitment to permanent change in the organization, a change that takes years to fully realize, then investment in adequate training becomes both necessary and small.

Training is so important, in fact, that in any organization, large or small, an installation program should include a full-time trainer, or at least a full-time advisor or program administrator who doubles as a trainer. It is not enough to send people to outside training courses or bring in temporary trainers. The role of trainer must exist as a full-time and permanent component of the quality circle office.

Many American companies fail to understand the significance of quality circle training. They regard it as a period of passive acceptance of new skills and knowledge. Employees *receive* training. Companies also shortsightedly regard training as a *nonproductive* period in which members are imbued with knowledge and skills which they will put to use productively during their regular working sessions. Finally, they view it in the narrow sense of *training*, rather than in the broad sense of *learning*.

In contrast, you should view all quality circle activities as a continuous educational process in which members train themselves. The formal training courses just get the process started. In fact, quality circles in Japan started as *study* groups. The emphasis was not on short-term output but on long-term gains. The emphasis was not on solving problems but on making long-term improvements through the study of methods to raise the quality and productivity of their work. Circle members spent and continue to spend much of their time studying techniques of statistical quality control and productivity improvement. And they do so actively. Their training has resulted in an ongoing, self-sustained process.

7

Preparing
the Organization

Quality circles cannot be understood outside the context of
the organization in which they exist. Similarly, they cannot
hope to succeed without an organization which will, as
Toyota Auto Body has demonstrated, encourage participation, support their needs, respond to their requests, and
measure their results. It is essential, then, that you develop
plans to prepare the organization before forming the first
circle.

Providing Incentives

An argument persists in the United States about the reasons employees participate in quality circles. One camp
feels that their motives are "intrinsic"—that employees
have basic needs for self-actualization and recognition, a
desire for meaningful participation, and so on. The opposite camp agrees that these motives are important, but be-
lieves that the major long-term motivator—and the only
"equitable" one—is money, an "extrinsic" motivator. Circles develop projects that save the organization huge sums
of money, they argue. Circle members should receive a
share of these savings.

Time is an important factor when trying to determine which employee incentives are appropriate. When a circle first begins, intrinsic motivators are very powerful. The right to participate in decisions affecting their work, to voice their views and demonstrate their worth, elicits heady enthusiasm from employees. In time, however, these factors lose their appeal. Quality circle activities become commonplace and routine, no longer capable of intrinsically motivating participation. Employees begin to ask "Where's the payoff? We spend months developing a cheaper way to do the job and the company says our reward is that we feel better. The president feels a whole lot better than we do. He gets a bonus when plant productivity increases."

To succeed in the long run, a quality circle effort must provide both nonfinancial *and* financial incentives for employees who participate. Quality circles will, by themselves, generate a great deal of interest and enthusiastic participation. But eventually excitement dwindles. When it does, the organization, guided by the quality circle office, must reward participants. There are a number of means for achieving this, and all of them should be utilized.

Recognition: Achievements of quality circles must be publicized in organizational newsletters and bulletins or posted on bulletin boards so that the participants receive acknowledgment from both management and their peers for their efforts.

Competition for recognition: Competition between circles rewards both members and the organization if it focuses on the quality of projects and management presentations. When a quality circle effort has developed sufficient momentum, an annual competition between circles greatly enhances employees' interest in participating. Of course, if rewards for winning are visible and substantial, participation will be that much greater.

The system of competition serves an even larger purpose if circles from different departments compete for company honors. In this way, general foremen and managers will acquire a stake in the outcome and be more willing to support the circles in their departments. In Japan, the Japanese Union of Scientists and Engineers has carried this one degree further by organizing a national competition in which circles representing different companies compete for top national honors.

Recognition outside the organization: Putting members, leaders, and advisors in contact with their counterparts in other organizations gives them a tremendous motivational boost. For example, you might encourage the formation of local chapters of the International Association of Quality Circles. These chapters publish quarterly newsletters and meet regularly to discuss quality and productivity improvements. You can also send circle members and advisors to annual conferences of the International Association of Quality Circles or any other organization that promotes presentations; this encourages members to feel part of a larger, meaningful movement and serves as a reward for their efforts.

Financial incentives: Financial incentives can be either indirect or direct. Bonus systems, based on overall performance of the employee (including quality circle participation along with other aspects of the job) as well as the company, offer one example of indirect financial incentives. The case of Toyota Auto Body illustrates a system of this type in which the bonus is calculated according to company performance and the employee's tenure and performance on the job, including quality circle participation.

Using a suggestion system to reward quality circle performance is an example of direct financial incentives. In this case, the circle simply becomes a group suggestor and its reward is based on an estimate of the amount of money its proposal will save the organization.

Another direct approach is similar to the standard profit-sharing plan. Circle members are directly rewarded for their role in solving a problem, but the cash is placed in funds that earn interest and are matched by the company according to its annual performance. Cash awards are determined either by a fixed rate or as a percent of estimated cost savings over a year. An employee can withdraw the money from his account at any time, but if he does so within the first two or three years, he forfeits the company matching funds. Obviously this approach has two advantages: it creates an additional cash fund from which the company can draw, and it provides a strong incentive for employees to stay with the company, thus reducing turnover.

Career advancement: The existence of a quality circle effort creates a new career hierarchy within the organization. Any installation program with full- or part-time advisors should be structured with the recognition that someday these roles may constitute career opportunities. That is, a member of a circle should be able to perceive that he or she might someday be a circle leader, then an advisor to another circle (if part-time) or to many circles (if full-time), then a trainer, and perhaps even an administrator.

There is little evidence to suggest that one system of incentives is demonstrably better than others. In fact, as the Toyota Auto Body example demonstrates, you should probably combine two or more to ensure good results. It would be a serious mistake not to provide some form of incentive for employees participating in quality circles. Incentives are important, and a quality circle effort will flounder without them.

A warning: Many people have the mistaken notion that

a program which must be reinforced by public recognition, competition for prestige, and financial rewards is artificial and invalid. They make the mistake of equating results with incentives. They believe that the only legitimate motivation is the intrinsic satisfaction of having done a good job. Anything else corrupts an endeavor.

Nothing could be further from the truth. Whatever the motivation, the result—participation in quality circles—is the important thing. Employees choose to participate for a variety of reasons. Your task is to provide a set of soundly structured incentives to ensure consistent participation.

Structuring Incentives

CASE #17
Competing with Suggestion Systems

As its first project, the mechanical assembly quality circle chose to redesign a workstand. They felt that the old one lacked stability, and the safety office agreed. A planner and a designer assisted them in their effort. Four months later they completed their project and presented it. After a great deal of discussion, delay, and difficulty, the new stand was delivered. It was not the most attractive piece of equipment in the shop, but it was stable and did the job. Proud of their first achievement, they turned to their second project.

Unknown to the circle, a quality inspector, after hearing them talk about the problem of the old stand and the need for a new one, submitted a suggestion for a new stand. The suggestion office accepted it and gave him a monetary reward for his idea. This happened at about the same time that the new stand was installed.

It didn't take long for the circle members to find out

about the award. Although they showed no emotion, they were furious. They felt that the quality circle office had made fools of them. They had contributed their time and effort, with nothing tangible in return, while the sly inspector had only to fill out a piece of paper to receive a handsome reward for work that they had done.

Understandably, over the next two months, participation in the circle declined. Once-loyal members found excuses not to attend. The advisor grew alarmed. He probed and questioned, but could find no real cause for the decline. Finally, in frustration, he provoked a response by becoming angry. He laid it on the line—either the group would attend the meetings and choose a new project that might benefit them—or he was not going to bother with them anymore.

At this point the group's anger surfaced. A woman, the most vocal member of the circle, said plainly that she saw no point in circle activities if an inspector could get credit and money for a job that other people did.

The advisor agreed that the complaint was legitimate. He contacted the suggestion coordinator and together they investigated the matter. Quality circle rules at the plant stipulated that the circle "owns" an idea or project on the date that it first appears in its minutes. A check revealed that the mention of the workstand first occurred on April 28, a Thursday. The suggestion records showed that the inspector heard the members discussing the problem in their work area on Monday or Tuesday and submitted his suggestion on Tuesday, two days before their regularly scheduled meeting. Though they thought of the project first, the circle members had not written it into their minutes until two or three days later.

Given this evidence and its obvious impact on the circle, the advisor and the suggestion coordinator decided, with the approval of the steering committee for the suggestion office, that the circle should submit their suggestion in writing. They did so and quickly received an award.

The members now saw that they could participate in circles and still enjoy the benefits of the suggestion system. But a new problem had developed, because they learned another lesson in the process—they could earn more by submitting suggestions individually than they could by submitting them as a group. The amount of the reward remained constant and, if the circle submitted a winning solution, the members had to divide the reward equally among themselves. This reduced a $100 payoff, for example, to a $10 payoff per person.

During the following weeks, the effects of this competition between the suggestion system and the quality circle became obvious. One of the members privately submitted two suggestions rather than handle the matter through the quality circle process. Another member, once vocal and active, remained silent in circle discussions. When asked why, he responded that he preferred not to speak because his ideas would belong to the circle and he could not submit them to the suggestion system for his own profit.

Worst of all, the members ceased to tackle problems constructively. Instead of isolating a problem and systematically analyzing it to determine the cause and develop a solution, they began to list possible solutions and submit them to the suggestion system. In short, they turned the quality circle process into a forum for generating suggestions rather than solving problems.

• • •

This tangle of incentives and rewards can get worse. Members can and will measure in dollars the advantages of suggestion systems versus quality circles. If payoffs are obviously greater for suggestions, members will choose the suggestion system and the quality circle process will suffer seriously.

Should you let the best system win? I think not. These are two entirely different systems and, while both contribute solutions and improvements, quality circles do a great deal more for the organization. They greatly improve employee attitudes about the organization and their role within it. They enhance a spirit of teamwork and instill an awareness of the importance of doing quality work. Statistics show that they reduce quality defects, improve productivity, and reduce the rates of grievances, attrition, and accidents. Suggestion systems do none of these things.

To defuse the potential conflict between the quality circle process and a suggestion system, automatically submit all quality circle proposals to the suggestion system and reward circles on a higher scale than that used to reward individuals. This ensures maximum participation in circles and reduces conflict between the two systems, while allowing them to coexist. Coexistence is important, because those people who will never want to participate in quality circles must always have available to them the option to submit individual suggestions. The higher scale used for rewarding circles tells employees in clear and unequivocal terms—in money—that the organization considers the circle process important.

Providing Technical Support

Providing technical support is one of the most difficult, but necessary, aspects of a quality circle effort. Circles cannot function if they do not have access to information and technical expertise. On the other hand, the manner in which technical support is provied can smother the spon-

taneous energy of members and destroy their effectiveness.

The Planner

A mechanical assembly crew on first shift decided to form
a circle composed of hourly employees, the supervisor,
and the key technical people with whom they interfaced
regularly. They reasoned that a group that included all the
key actors—mechanics, supervisor, engineer, planner, and
quality inspector—could solve problems more quickly than
a group composed merely of mechanics and their supervisor.

In the early meetings, following training, they focused
on a rather complex problem: proving the inadequacy of
their drill tools and demonstrating the cost effectiveness of
buying newer, more advanced tools. The project served
the needs of the hourly members directly, because they
spent many hours wrestling with broken drill bits and ir-
regular holes.

As the group set about the task of collecting evidence
on lost time, broken tools, repair time, and repair costs, a
problem began to surface. In meeting after meeting, conversation was monopolized by the planner. He seemed to
have a need to talk, and when he was not talking to the
group as a whole, he was addressing himself to the engineer, as though the engineer were the only person capable of understanding him.

Most of the hourly employees deferred to his apparent
expertise and remained silent. After all, he was a salaried
technical expert being paid to have answers. Interestingly,
when he was not present, they had a great deal to say about
the many problems they were having with tools. They had

many ideas about what kind of tool would be best. They revealed complications not previously discussed. Clearly, without consciously intending to do so, the planner was intimidating the hourly members, and they, in turn, were allowing it to happen.

As time went on, the hourly workers grew frustrated. They began to argue with the planner over every issue. He, in response, took to playing devil's advocate no matter how obvious and useful the proposal was. He indulged in long dissertations on technical points to demonstrate his expertise, and he sidetracked every conversation that seemed to favor the hourly members' point of view. Clearly, a subtle undercurrent of hostility was growing. The hourly employees were determined to be heard, while the planner, threatened by what he saw as a challenge to his authority, fought to control the circle by having the last word on everything.

Eventually, the circle was irrevocably damaged by this hidden battle. The older members grew tired of the struggle and retreated behind time-honored defenses, mumbling about "company men." Even the younger members eventually stopped attending, leaving only the supervisor and the salaried members. Finally, when a slack period developed and the members were transferred to other shops, they took the face-saving opportunity to declare the circle disbanded.

. . .

The consequences of directly involving technical experts in quality circles are obvious. They tend to dominate the group, and are defensive about maintaining their authority. The ideas of the members are never heard and their need to participate freely is never satisfied.

A better solution to the problem of providing technical support is to prohibit full circle membership for technical specialists, but to require that they attend circle meetings when requested by the members. This allows the members to control the interaction by calling in technical advice when it is needed and dismissing it once the necessary information has been supplied.

In larger organizations, it might be wise to follow the example of Toyota Auto Body and form a technical support committee charged with responding to circle requests for information and advice. But, here again, the critical idea is to offer assistance only when it is requested. Do not force advice on the circles. Simply make it available.

Should these two methods of providing technical support prove to be inadequate, a third can be added, but only after the quality circle process has been established in your organization. Create a centrally located project board or regularly circulated project list. This board or list announces the topics that each circle is currently dealing with and invites all interested persons to contact the circle.

A warning: Too much technical assistance can kill a circle's initiative. Technical support groups instinctively seek control over all decisions relating to their expertise. They do not want to support so much as to control. While their input is necessary to a successful quality circle process, you must always guard against too much technical support. A crude solution hammered out by circle members themselves is better than a technically elegant solution for which the members feel no ownership.

Following Up

Quality circles engage in a two-stage process. The first stage involves employees. They identify a problem, analyze it, and devise and present a solution in a well-reasoned and well-supported fashion to management. The second stage involves managers. They listen to the presentation, evaluate the proposal, and decide—often after a second or third meeting—whether or not to implement it. If the decision is favorable, they devise a plan to put the proposal into effect and implement it as quickly as possible. The process comes full circle as the members monitor the success of their proposal back in their work area.

A major pitfall for the quality circle process, and one seldom anticipated, is the failure of management and the organization in general to implement the proposal without needless delay. When this happens, the members soon abandon their circles.

CASE #19
The Glove Box

A group of electrical cable fabricators, all of them women, formed a circle. Their supervisor had an intuitive grasp of the quality circle concept and soon became an able leader. She controlled the regular meetings firmly, but never dominated them. Participation was strong, and the circle quickly produced its first proposal, which concerned the problems created by their need to cover some of their cable assemblies with a protective material composed primarily of fiberglass. Whenever they did this, they got bits of fiberglass on their hands, arms, and faces—despite protective clothing and masks. Some of it even got into their eyes and down their throats. To protect themselves, they devised a "glove box," a sealed plastic box with rubber gloves inserted into it. They reasoned that the best thing to do was to isolate the fiberglass, rather than bury themselves in more protective clothing. They presented their proposal and, after discussion of the costs, management agreed to implement it.

For a couple of weeks both members and management

were content in the knowledge that a problem had been solved and soon a glove box would appear in the electrical fabrication shop. After two months, however, the supervisor began to wonder whether any progress was in fact being made. She called around and discovered, much to her surprise, that no one in the planning department, in tool design, or in tool control had any information about the project. It didn't exist. Management had approved the solution, but no paperwork had been initiated to get it implemented!

• • •

This may seem unlikely, but it is a common occurrence. The electrical fabricators were lucky. They called the plant manager to complain, and he himself ordered the glove box constructed. Going to the top, however, is not a proper solution, because the tracking and implementation of proposals gets built in to the functions of the quality circle office rather than becoming institutionalized in the full quality circle process. Should this happen, the office may well become a separate hierarchy with its own constituency—quality circles—and its own rewards to dispense—response to proposals. And thus the regular hierarchy is bypassed and undermined.

The quality circle office must promote an institutionalized system of effective and timely follow-up for each quality circle proposal. There are two good solutions. First, the office can promote the formation of a committee of managers representing each major department. The committee would meet regularly to review the progress of circle proposals and assign implementation responsibilities. This approach has the advantages of involving the widest number of people, thus spreading ownership of the program throughout the organization. On the other hand, it has all the drawbacks of a committee.

A second solution is to appoint someone within a strategic department—long-range planning for example—with the specific responsibility for tracking the progress of circle proposals and ensuring that they are implemented quickly and completely. This solution has the disadvantages of concentrating the responsibility in one spot, thus limiting ownership. Still, what is lost in terms of organizational participation may be balanced by increased efficiency.

Whichever solution is chosen, either of these two or perhaps an altogether different approach particularly suited to your organization, it is important that the quality circle office begin promoting and preparing a mechanism for quick follow-up before the first circle is formed. This is especially important in organizations where middle management is expected to resist the quality circle process, for it is in the process of implementing proposals that middle managers can squelch or alter a proposal even after they have publicly accepted it.

CASE #20
Attempted Sabotage

A group from the paint shop had a problem with contamination of aluminum. After a number of months they were able to isolate some of the causes, which were related to inadequate control of the atmosphere in the shop. Between cleaning and painting, dust particles were settling on the panels. To solve the problem, they decided to propose that an enclosed, atmospherically controlled preparation room be built in one corner of their shop. With the help of facilities engineering, they drew up plans for the room and made a presentation.

The proposal was well received by the manager of their department as well as the supervisors. It gave them something they needed but did not have. Only the general foreman seemed reluctant, but he voiced no opposition.

A week after the presentation, the foreman went to the manager of the facilities department and argued that the room was both unnecessary and expensive. He was, in effect, trying to sabotage the project. The facilities manager alone could not stop the project, but he agreed to propose to the facilities department that it be abandoned.

Fortunately the advisor to the circle learned of the plot and went to the manager of the general foreman. The manager, in turn, called in the general foreman and asked him why he fought the project when it was obviously a good idea. The general foreman attempted to argue that the room was not needed, but eventually admitted that he just could not tolerate the idea of his employees telling him what needed to be done. The manager warned the foreman not to interfere again and ordered the room built.

•   •   •

Many of the problems that arise in the course of implementing circle projects are resolved by forming leader circles and leader councils, because when general foremen and supervisors are involved directly in circle activities of their own, they see for themselves what the benefits are and they work avidly to see the projects implemented.

Measuring Results

Sooner or later it happens with every quality circle effort: the boss calls and wants to see written results. If you are not prepared, the meeting can be embarrassing. But justifying your quality circles to budget-minded managers is not the only reason to measure circle results. You must do it to sell the concept to skeptics, to guide your installation efforts, and, ultimately, to provide feedback to supervisors and circle members so that they can better fulfill their roles in the quality circle process.

The quality circle office must institute a solid system of measurement *before* forming circles in order to have a baseline against which to measure achievements. You must decide which measures to use, who will gather the data, and how and when they will gather it. You must decide how to analyze it and how to display it.

Four basic types of data are to be collected: installation program results, circle outputs, organizational outcomes, and personal outcomes.

Installation program results: These are simple measures of the scope and pace of the installation effort. They include such things as:

- Number of supervisor-leaders trained.
- Number of employee-members trained.
- Number of circles formed.
- Success rates (number of active circles over the total number of circles formed, number of active members over the total number of members trained, and number of active leaders over the total number of supervisors trained).
- Volunteer rate (number of employees joining a circle over the number of employees who received a presentation on quality circles and the opportunity to join).
- Participation rates (number of members over the total number of employees, and number of leaders over the total number of supervisors).

Circle outputs: These are the manifest products of circle activities. They include:

- Number of management presentations.
- Types of proposals presented (for example, quality defect reductions and productivity improvements).
- Presentation rate (number of presentations per circle per year).
- Approval rate (number of proposals accepted by management).

Organizational outcomes: These are the various effects of quality circles on the organization. They include:

- Change in production rates.
- Change in defect rates.
- Change in scrap rates.
- Change in attrition rates.
- Change in lost time rates.
- Change in grievance rates.
- Change in accident rates.
- Estimated cost savings (total estimated cost savings resulting from approved proposals, and estimates of savings from organizational outcomes).
- Ratio of cost savings to program expenditures.

Personal outcomes: These are changes in employee attitudes that can be related to participation in quality circles. They usually include assessments of the attitudes of employees toward:

- The quality circle process.
- Their jobs.
- Themselves.
- Their co-workers.
- Their supervisors.
- Their management in general.
- The organization in general.

Installation program results and circle outcomes need no further discussion. They are straightforward statistics that all quality circle offices should maintain. Organizational outcomes and personal outcomes, however, are more complex. Consequently, they require greater understanding of what you wish to demonstrate, what unit of measure you should choose, who should collect the raw data, and when the data should be collected.

Organizational outcomes: A tight, rigorous test of the organizational changes engendered by quality circles requires the simultaneous comparison of two dimensions: (1) the performance of individuals (rates of quality defects, productivity, and so on) within a group of quality circle members before they join circles, and (2) the performance of a group of quality circle members with a group of nonmembers doing the same work. Combined, these dimensions of contrast produce a four-square paradigm as shown in Figure 1.

When the squares—A, B, C, and D—are filled with real data,* the results may appear as shown in Figure 2, which shows clearly that, while the quality circle members performed at a worse rate than nonmembers before they joined circles, they outperformed nonmembers by .1 defects per person (D−C) after they joined circles. It also shows that, while nonmembers improved by .1 defects per person, or 25 percent [(B−D)/B], members improved by .29 defects per person, or 59 percent [(A−C)/A]. Thus, we can say that quality circle members outperformed nonmembers by 34 percent during the test period of six months.

These results allow a quality circle office to convince the most skeptical critic and to claim credit for a very siza-

---

* The data used in Figure 2 are from the Martin Marietta Corporation experience cited in Chapter 1. See Tortorich et al., op. cit.

FIGURE 1

Quality Circle

	Member	Nonmember
Before Joining	A	B
After Joining	C	D

FIGURE 2

Quality Circle

	Member	Nonmember
Before Joining	A .49	B .40
After Joining	C .20	D .30

ble improvement throughout the organization. Most important, if the quality circle effort must justify its existence in terms of return on investment, these hard numbers can be translated into dollars saved, added to the estimated cost savings from circle projects, and weighed against dollars spent on promoting and maintaining quality circles. If it collects its data carefully, a quality circle office can claim credit for dollars saved through reduced rates of attrition, lost time, accidents, defects, and scrap, and improved productivity. To these figures it can add estimated savings that would result when circle proposals are implemented.

Figure 2 represents an ideal situation. Unfortunately, the realities of quality circle installation make it difficult to collect such figures. The major problem is that circles are constantly formed, thus removing people from the nonmember column and placing them in the member column. Similarly, time marches on, and with new circles being formed each month, the "before" period for all circles varies. And of course not all circles complete their "after" period at the same time. In short, the membership in the four squares is in a constant state of flux.

Despite these difficulties, it is possible to achieve these comparisons by making a number of assumptions and carefully balancing groups and time periods.*

If you find it impossible to develop these models for measuring performance, the easier thing is to compare the performance of circle members with that of nonmembers on a regular basis, usually every month. Figure 3 shows how to display these kinds of data.

As most of the employees join circles, comparisons between members and nonmembers and "before" and "after" become meaningless. And as there are fewer and

---

* The procedure for doing so is too involved to present here. For a good example of how it is done in one quality circle program see Tortorich et al., op. cit.

FIGURE 3

Rate of logged accidents per person per month for quality circle members and nonmembers. (Source: Tortorich et. al.)

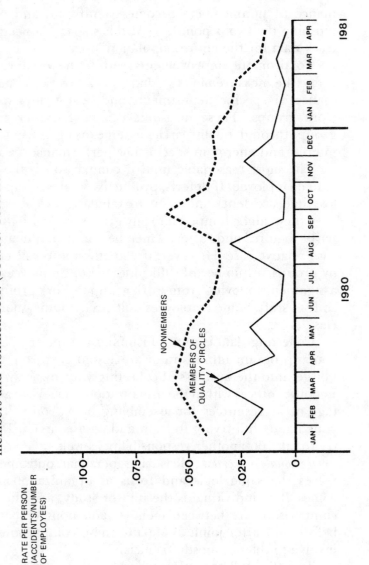

fewer nonmembers, the effect of members on the performance of nonmembers becomes significant, and distin-
guishing the two is pointless. At this stage, you need only
track data for the entire population.

To promote improvements within the organization,
refine the measurements so that you can track the performance of specific departments and, eventually, specific
work groups. These measures can be fed back to the
groups through quality circles as a means of focusing their
interest and energy in specific low performance areas.

The most reasonable unit of comparison is the individual employee. If defects, productivity rates, scrap rates,
lost time, accidents, and so on are tabulated by individuals,
then they can be lumped into any groups you wish to compare ("before" and "after," "member" and "nonmember")
with relative ease. However, if you attempt to collect data
by groups, a number of difficulties arise. Employees shift
assignments, moving from work group to work group and
shift to shift. Some employees quit circles. Others join circles.

Collecting data is time consuming and boring. Unless
you as program administrator are absolutely forced to, do
not get into the business of collecting your own raw data.
Let other offices within the organization do it. Take advantage of its resources for assembling data. You will have
your hands full trying to train and advise circles. Do not
try to take on another responsibility as well.

Personal outcomes: Measuring personal outcomes involves the same logic and focus as organizational outcomes. The individual is the unit of study, and the basic
comparisons are between member and nonmember and
before and after joining. Making these comparisons can
involve problems, mostly financial.

To collect all the information needed to make these
comparisons, you can develop or obtain a test instru-

ment—a questionnaire—that measures the attitudes you consider relevant and apply it to all employees, first before any quality circles are formed and then at regular intervals thereafter, perhaps every six months or every year.

Developing an attitude questionnaire can be expensive and time consuming. Even a purchased questionnaire may cost a great deal of time and money to administer and to tabulate. Most important, administering and tabulating a questionnaire can become a full-time job, consuming energy that ought to be devoted to training and advising quality circles.

Thus, if your organization already has an attitude questionnaire that it applies regularly, use it as a source of raw data. If not, enter the realm of questionnaires with caution. Probably the easiest thing to do is to purchase a simple attitude questionnaire that measures the kinds of things mentioned previously under the heading of "personal outcomes" and apply it only to prospective circle members before they receive a presentation on circles and at regular intervals thereafter. Of course, a simple questionnaire of this type lacks the ability to compare members to nonmembers, but it does provide for a "before" and "after" test, and it has the ability to note trends and monitor attitudes of participating employees while avoiding the often monumental task of administering and tabulating an organizationwide questionnaire at regular intervals.

8
Working Out
the Details

After choosing an installation strategy, developing the necessary training courses, and preparing the organization, you are ready to recruit and train quality circles. At this point, numerous questions arise. Many of them are peculiar to specific organizations, some are common to all Here are the more important ones and suggested ways of dealing with them.

Forming a Circle

Determining a target group: Where should you form the first circles? Should you choose an area with definite problems or one that works smoothly? Should the circle involve supervisors who perform well, or should it focus on supervisors with problems?

Because quality circles are difficult to develop and, at first, are very fragile, begin with a department or shop where employees have a reputation for quality work and the relations between supervisors and employees are positive. In short, choose an area with the highest probability of success, not one where the circles will have to overcome a history of conflict and poor workmanship. Later, when the quality circle process has proved its value to the organization, introduce circles into the problem areas.

This advice may seem obvious, but many program administrators, managers, directors, and plant managers all assume that quality circles function as band-aids. They try to use them to overcome specific trouble spots in the organization without realizing that the circle process represents a more fundamental change in the entire organization.

One large and well-known firm on the West Coast should serve as an example of what not to do. This company surveyed an entire department, looking for hostile and nonproductive relations between supervisor and employees. After locating just such a department, the management privately confronted the supervisors with the results of the survey and strongly suggested that they do something to correct the situation, offering quality circles as the cure.

There is no information available on the outcome of the firm's quality circle effort. Presumably it met with some success. But obviously this approach places an unfair burden on the quality circle concept by asking it not only to solve employees' work-related problems but also to solve complex human relations problems.

Approaching the target group: Once you choose a target group, the next step is to approach it correctly. Here the middle-down strategy comes into play. Remember, the essential objective is to spread the sense of ownership in such a way that middle management and supervision, as well as employees, feel that quality circles belong to them and can meet their needs.

Contact managers or general foremen directly, face-to-face, and acquaint them with the quality circle concept. A presentation of specific results, such as reduced defects, reduced lost time, reduced accidents, and improved productivity, encourages acceptance. Once they are familiar with the concept, ask them to attend a training course for managers and technical specialists to learn more about their role in the quality circle process and how they might utilize quality circles in their department.

Once managers and general foremen have completed the course, ask them to recommend supervisors for the leader training course. Contact the supervisors, acquaint them with the concept, and ask them to attend the course. When they have completed it, have the supervisor and an advisor promote the formation of circles. For maximum impact, and to make sure that everyone sees and understands that management supports the quality circle effort, have the manager, general foreman, and supervisor attend the meeting in which a circle is formed. Let the manager and general foreman open the meeting with strong statements about the importance of circles and affirming their support.

Another approach is to contact managers and general foremen and ask them to recommend supervisors for the leader training course, leaving the manager training course for a time when there is a sufficient number of participating managers to warrant such a course. Either way, the essential idea is that you contact managers and supervisors first, before contacting employees.

Forming a circle: After recruiting and training managers and supervisors, you need to recruit members. Proceed cautiously. Employees may misinterpret the concept and supervisors will distort it if you are not clear and consistent in your presentation to all groups.

The meeting to form a circle should be obligatory. In that meeting, the supervisor and the advisor present the quality circle concept, its benefits for the employees and the organization, and the rules of the quality circle process in the organization. Allow plenty of time for questions and discussion. At the end of the presentation, reiterate the voluntary nature of quality circles: employees are not forced to join, they may resign at any time if they wish, and they may postpone the decision to join. Then announce when training will begin and invite those who wish to participate to contact the supervisor before the starting date.

This procedure helps ensure that the supervisor becomes the circle leader and that membership is strictly voluntary. It also helps avoid the very common situation in which a supervisor tries to handpick the members. And it helps to overcome the tendency for circles to form around exclusive networks or cliques. All employees learn from the beginning that they may join or resign at any time without restrictions that are based on training or selection by supervisor or election by active members.

Determining circle structure: Up to this point, our frame of reference has been the ideal quality circle—a supervisor and volunteers from among that supervisor's employees. In its early stages, for the first couple of years, a quality circle office should try to promote circles that fit this pattern. It stays well within the bounds of the existing control structure of an organization and therefore poses little threat. The quality circle office must also remain flexible, however. Once members of an organization grasp the possibilities for changing the system, they will want to modify and expand the concept. These attempts to innovate should not be resisted, but before you venture into them, understand what might happen and how the variations from the standard model may affect the success of the quality circle effort in the organization.

Task force circles: The most common variation in circle

structure defines membership according to a single problem. That is, a problem is chosen and circle members are selected according to their relationship to the problem (see Diagram 11).

CASE #21
A Task Force Circle

A general foreman in the finance department identified a serious problem in his department that concerned two other departments—personnel and materials. The paperwork system for handling the assignment of new employees and the relocation of transferred employees would frequently break down, producing a long list of problems—delays in the arrival of personal possessions, delays in payments of relocation allowances, incorrect payments, and so on.

The foreman proposed the formation of a quality circle with members drawn from key positions in each of the three departments. The quality circle office agreed, waiving the normal procedures for selection of members. It also trained the general foreman as the circle leader and helped to train the members he selected.

The circle quickly went to work. The members developed a detailed diagram of the paper flow for relocation and used it to isolate problem areas. They focused on each problem, analyzing it in detail. They also developed an "ideal" system and worked backward to the problems of the existing system. When they finished their analysis, they were able to identify solutions that, though they did not embody the ideal system, effectively solved their problems at reasonable costs. Members implemented most of the solutions on their own authority and eventually made a presentation to upper management to show what they had

DIAGRAM 11
Task force quality circle.

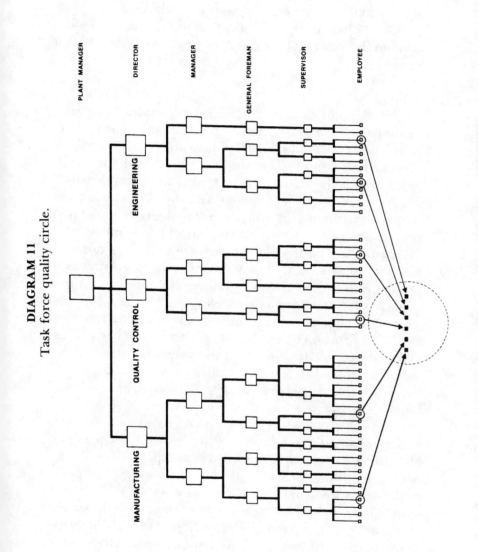

done and to ask for approval of a number of the major innovations requiring changes in procedures.

Once they completed their project, the circle disbanded, having no other common problem to justify their existence.

• • •

This kind of circle structure has tremendous problem-solving power. Formal, hierarchical organizations isolate people in individual job functions within departments or offices that communicate fairly well internally, but hardly at all externally. In this context, employees immediately see the value of getting together with their counterparts in other departments to work out problems that seemed nearly impossible to solve through normal channels.

On the less positive side, task force circles are not permanent. They exist to deal with only one or possibly two problems and then they fade away. For this reason, the quality circle office would do well to encourage all supervisors and employees to form the basic quality circle first and then form task force circles on an *ad hoc* basis. This makes it possible for members to participate regularly in their "home-base" circle and form, in addition, a task force circle to solve a specific, complicated problem involving other departments.

Professional association circles: Another variation in circle structure is best described as a "professional association." Most quality circles are composed of a supervisor and volunteers from among his employees, where everyone works in the same work area for the same boss. In the professional circle, the membership is composed of individuals who perform the same job function, but in different shops or departments and under different bosses (see Diagram 12). A circle of secretaries is the most common example.

DIAGRAM 12
Professional association quality circle.

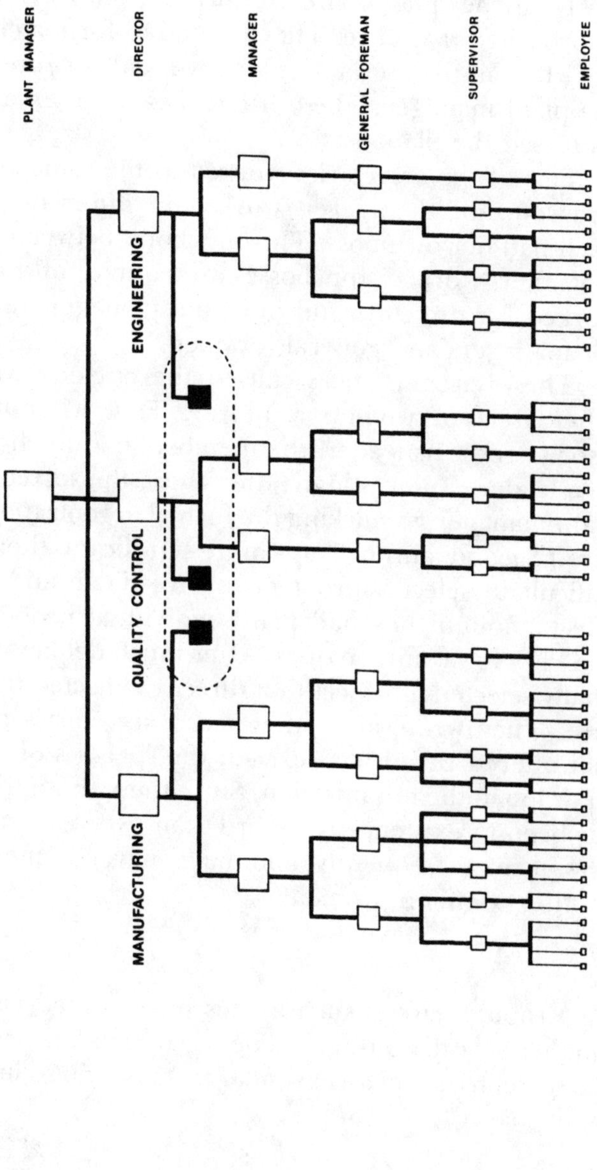

CASE #22
The Secretaries

Early in the quality circle effort, a group of secretaries approached the office. They wanted to form a circle composed of all the secretaries who worked for directors and the plant manager. The office had some reservations, but endorsed the plan.

Few of the secretaries worked in the same work area, and some of them even worked in different buildings. Each had her own boss. The only bond between them was that they worked for bosses of equivalent rank—they worked for directors and the plant manager, rather than for managers and general foremen.

These circumstances caused the circle to vary from other circles in two important ways. First, without a supervisor to serve as leader, the members had to choose their own leader. (Interestingly, they chose the secretary to the plant manager, mimicking the formal organizational structure.) Second, and perhaps more significant, they found it difficult to select a problem to investigate and solve. In effect, though they had many individual problems, they had very few common ones. After much deliberation, they finally selected a project that directly reflected their structure. They wrote and published a secretary's handbook that offered practical help with the specifics of the secretary's job in the organization. Since then, though the circle has been in existence for more than two years, the members meet infrequently and have never come up with another common problem.

. . .

Although circles such as this have limited value, they should not be discouraged. They accommodate people who, like secretaries, perform similar tasks but do so in isolation from each other. Quality inspectors and key-punch operators have much the same situation.

It is difficult to integrate people with such jobs into the ideal quality circle structure. Because their duties differ from the duties of the other members, quality inspectors and key-punch operators, for example, have no great interest in the circle's activities. Their problems are not those of the office workers or manufacturing workers who share the same work area. If the circle tries to accommodate these odd members, the result is not much better. The only common problems they can identify are usually the amorphous and unworkable ones that come under the heading of communications. Putting these roles into an ideal circle structure can actually hinder its development. Thus, it is wise to allow—even encourage—secretaries, quality inspectors, key-punch operators, and any other isolated job functions to form their own professional association circles.

Integrated circles: In some instances, two or more departments, even interfacing agencies, find it useful to form a circle to work on a large complex problem. Members are drawn from various levels of the interfacing departments and agencies, giving representation to everyone involved in the area under discussion (see Diagram 13).

CASE #23
An Integrated Circle

A large industrial corporation that produced hardware for a single customer, the government, had a difficult set of problems with its weld program. Too many defects occurred on certain welds, too many deadlines came and went without being met. To make matters worse, each weld had to be tracked and accepted by no fewer than three representatives: the company's quality inspector, the

DIAGRAM 13
Integrated quality circle.

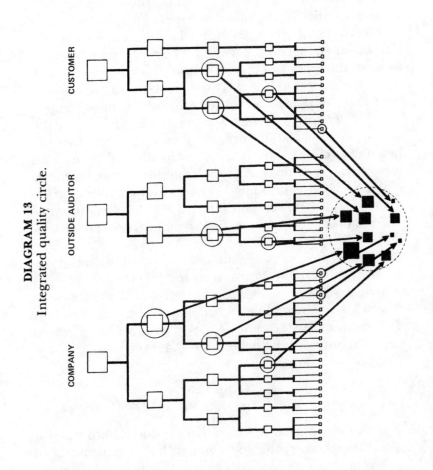

customer, and an outside auditor. The inspector challenged the manufacturing department. The auditor challenged both the inspector and manufacturing.

Though the magnitude of the problem clearly indicated that the individual welders were not responsible, they took the brunt of the blame. Morale plummeted and problems increased. Paper piled on top of paper, defects continued, and frustration mounted.

Finally, a customer representative proposed that a committee or board look into the problem and work out a solution. He approached the quality circle office in search of sponsorship. The office took up the challenge and helped him promote a special circle composed of representatives from the company's manufacturing department (two welders, a weld engineer, a welding supervisor, a general foreman, and a manager), the quality department (a quality engineer, a quality inspector, and a quality general foreman), the auditing group (two inspectors and a general foreman), and the customer (who initiated the idea). All the members received training in group problem-solving techniques and agreed to the standard process of identifying the problem, analyzing its causes, developing solutions, and presenting the results to a higher authority for review and acceptance.

In their first meeting after training, the group brainstormed nearly twenty major problems in the welding process. Then they identified three critical problems and assigned them the highest priority. They decided what required action and proceeded at once to make the changes that they alone had the authority to enact. With the preliminaries out of the way, they systematically began to analyze their three problems in depth and to develop long-term solutions to be presented to the company, the customer, and the auditor.

Four months later, when they had hammered out solutions to the problems, they presented their recommendations to the upper management of the company, the customer, and the auditor. They proposed new gap requirements for the welds, new weld schedules, and a new system of welder training, certification, and recertification.

All three proposals were accepted, and the integrated circle moved on to the consideration of the next two problems on its list—paperwork and weld tools.

• • •

This variation in circle structure requires some caution. It is a powerful problem-solving tool but it applies only to large, clustered problems that require complicated solutions. Because it varies considerably from the ideal circle structure, it requires careful monitoring from the quality circle office to ensure that it does not distort or corrupt the intent of the quality circle process. Like the problem-defined circle, the integrated circle lasts only as long as the cluster of problems remains unsolved. Once its task is complete, the circle is disbanded. And, like the problem-defined circle, it should be held in reserve—a structure that can be proposed when ideal circles uncover problems that require special organizational solutions.

There is one great advantage to integrated circles, whether they include members from different organizations or from different branches of the same organization: They involve middle managers directly in the quality circle process. Thus, an integrated circle gives middle managers firsthand experience as circle members, and if their circle is successful, they usually become strong advocates, rather than enemies, of the circle process.

Interorganizational circles: The principle of the integrated circle can be extended one step further to involve two or more separate organizations, as shown in Diagram 14.

DIAGRAM 14
Interorganizational quality circle.

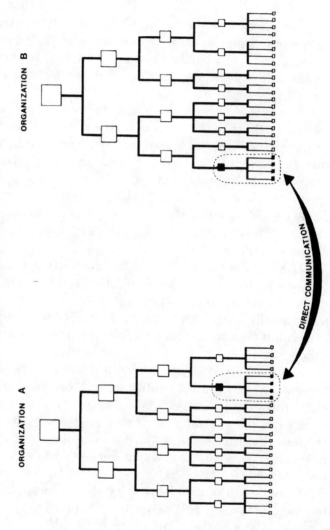

CASE #24
Interorganizational Cooperation

The employees of the mechanical assembly department, who worked on a specific section of an aircraft assembly, decided to form a circle. They received their training and began to work on a tooling problem that had bothered them for years.

One of the vice presidents of the company realized that all materials that the members assembled in their area originated with a single supplier. He suggested that the quality circle office, which was training the members and their supervisor-leader, try to convince the supplier to form a circle among those employees who produced the materials. With both circles in place, they could communicate problems to each other and work on mutually beneficial solutions.

The supplier agreed, and after convincing the union, the members of the new circle received training and began their regular meetings. They focused on their own problems, but like their sister circle, they were informed that they could take advantage of a telephone contact any time they wished.

Months passed. The mechanical assemblers worked steadily on their tooling problems, and showed little interest in the supplier circle. Then, as a result of various difficulties with incoming materials, the assembler circle realized that they were dealing with problems that originated with the supplier and that the supplier circle should be informed.

They listed the problems, telephoned the members of the supplier circle, and asked for solutions. Approached directly by peers, the supplier circle members responded with interest and energy. Within one week they called back with solutions and agreed to implement them. The problems were solved.

• • •

Here, as with the integrated and task force circles, advantages abound. But there may also be disadvantages. Solutions are often difficult to implement. One organization may approve of cooperating as long as the money saved is its own, but when the solution saves the other organization money and costs the first organization, cooperation may fade. The projects mentioned in the case just presented suffered this fate. The supplier eventually refused to implement the proposed improvements without a change in the contract to cover the cost of implementation.

Scheduling Circle Meetings

Inevitably, in every quality circle, problems arise with respect to the scheduling of meetings.

CASE #25
Scheduling

When production welders first formed their circle, they chose 9 A.M. Monday morning as a meeting time. Within two weeks they realized their mistake: early Monday morning no one was alert. They changed their time to 1 P.M. Thursday afternoon.

Things went well for the next two weeks, but the general foreman abruptly canceled the fifth session just before the meeting time, insisting that there was an urgent job to be done. In fact, there was no urgent job, and the members sat idle for an hour. A week later the same thing happened. The week after that the members were caught in a long weld cycle and could not meet.

In the next session, which was held as scheduled, the members began to complain bitterly. With justification, they claimed that the organization had lied to them. They had been told they would have one hour each week to work on job-related problems, yet the meeting was canceled week after week. If the situation were not reversed, they would be forced to conclude that the quality circle process was a joke. They would quit the circle.

In response to this indictment, the advisor insisted that the circle, its leader, and the general foreman get together to set a meeting time that would be least likely to conflict with the production schedule.

A cause-and-effect diagram of the problem of canceled meetings revealed that the production schedule always piled up at the end of the week. Moreover, they recognized that they regularly broke for a half-hour lunch at noon. With these two facts, they set their regular meeting time for 12:30, right after lunch, on Monday. The advisor succeeded in impressing upon the general foreman that he alone could not cancel a meeting. If the schedule piled up so that the circle could not meet at 12:30 on Monday, he should consult with the circle leader and the supervisor to reschedule the meeting for a convenient time later in the week. The general foreman stated his agreement before all the members.

• • •

If circle members work on an assembly line in a continuous process, the meeting time must obviously be set after working hours and will require special arrangements. If the circle members do not work on a continuous process assembly line, they will still encounter scheduling problems. If members analyze the work flow in their area, they can determine the hour that least affects their schedule. Once they choose an hour, their management should be asked to agree to it.

A meeting may be canceled because management, in the person of either the general foreman or the manager, decides that the regular production schedule takes precedence over the meeting. This is a difficult situation to handle. The manager or general foreman must have flexibility to cancel a meeting, but most managers and foremen abuse it. Moreover, some use it as a conscious tactic to sabotage quality circles, knowing that repeated cancellations of meetings will destroy a circle.

Time and again, the holding of regular meetings becomes the battleground on which the quality circle office and middle managers struggle over the existence of quality circles. To win, the office must insist on employees' rights to meet one hour each week. It must establish the policy that regular meetings must be *rescheduled* if the workload or schedule interferes. Under no circumstances can anyone other than members cancel meetings. If members lose that privilege, they lose ownership and will quickly conclude that management lied when it promised to grant one hour each week for them to work on problems of their choice.

Leading Circle Meetings

The program administrator, trainers, and advisors spend most of their time trying to support and build effective circle leadership. This activity leads to a major problem: if any of them is overzealous and domineering, he or she may be drawn into the role of leader. To guard against this, the office must make it clear at the outset that only the

..₃or or an employee can be the circle leader. Members and managers must understand that all quality circles are obligated to follow this rule.

Another problem plagues circles, particularly in the early stages. The supervisor frequently cannot attend the meetings, leaving leadership in a vacuum. To overcome this difficulty, the office should rule that the secretary assumes the leader role in the leader's absence, or that the supervisor will designate a substitute leader. The members could also choose their own substitute leader by vote. Whatever path, there must be a second in command to take over in the leader's absence.

Choosing Problems and Projects

Too often managers, general foremen, and supervisors feel that they and they alone can and should determine what employees do in quality circles. To counteract this tendency, the office must indicate clearly that circle members choose their own topics. Like voluntarism, the right of members to choose the problems they wish to solve and the improvements they wish to make is fundamental to the success of quality circles. The office must ensure that no one usurps this right.

Although circle members have the right to choose their problem or project, they can do so only within certain limits. Topics must remain within the general category of what is work-related. For example, they cannot deal with home life or politics. They cannot deal with items that the personnel department and the union typically handle. They cannot develop a project dealing with salaries, wages, benefits, grievances, or job classifications, and they cannot delve into matters of personality. In short, they must stick to issues and systems.

These regulations serve very clear purposes. The restriction to work-related topics concentrates circle members on items that are relevant to the organization or, at least, are not detrimental to it. Restrictions against discussing salaries, wages, benefits, grievances, and job classifications prevent them from becoming a kind of mini union and usurping the functions of the union. The prohibition against dealing with personalities prevents them from engaging in witchhunts and character assassinations. The office, and particularly the advisor, must make sure that everyone understands these rules and must aggressively intervene when they are violated. Experience shows that members will readily agree to such rules as long as they are stated clearly in advance so that there are no erroneous expectations.

Requesting Information

There are two sources from which circles can request information: those inside the organization and those outside the organization.

Inside the organization: To function effectively, quality circles must have access to any information relevant to the problem or improvement on which they are working. If a group decides to improve the method of drilling holes in an assembly, for example (see Case #1), circle members have the right, and the duty, to contact engineering to obtain the relevant drawings; quality control to acquire statistics on defective holes; industrial engineering to learn the costs of the old method and determine the costs of the proposed method. With any restriction of this information the circle is incapable of developing and justifying a better method and the quality circle process is meaningless.

The best way to obtain needed advice or information is

for the circle to invite the key specialist to a regular meeting. This has the psychological advantage of bringing the specialist onto their home turf, rather than the other way around. It also utilizes available time most effectively, particularly if the specialist is informed of their needs and comes adequately prepared.

If this approach proves impossible, the circle can request information in writing, or it can visit the specialist in his office or work area. Both of these techniques are usually less effective than inviting the specialist directly to the meeting.

From time to time, a specialist refuses a circle's request for information or fails to respond to a circle's invitation. When this occurs, the quality circle office must intercede quickly and decisively to demonstrate to the specialist the advantages of working with circle members. If he persists in his disregard of the circle, the office must demand that he respond and back up this demand with the threat and, ultimately, the ability to go above him.

Blocking access to information can so hinder a circle's activities as to render the exercise meaningless and cause it to fail, but nontheless certain restrictions are necessary and must be stated and enforced. For example, quality circles cannot obtain personnel records or company proprietary information on such matters as patents and profits. These issues seldom arise in the course of a problem analysis and solution, but they can, and the quality circle office should be prepared to handle the situation.

CASE #26
Personnel Records

While preparing their proposal to form teams of welders and tool builders to visit suppliers in order to inspect tools before shipment to the plant, the tool fabrication quality circle (see Case #3) felt that they needed data on the qualifications of the quality department representatives in the field. They were convinced that these representatives could not do the inspection because they did not have the required skills and experience. The circle wanted to prove it with the facts from the personnel department. They wanted to compare the skills and experience of the representative with the skills and experience of their members. They wanted to make the point that a two-man team composed of a welder and a tool builder could assist the representative and fill in his lack of hands-on skill and knowledge.

The quality department and the personnel department refused to turn over files containing personal information. However, to accommodate the circle and to facilitate their proposal, the quality department tabulated average educational backgrounds and hands-on experience, as well as number of years as representatives, against which the circle members were able to make their case.

· · ·

Outside the organization: The freedom to talk to organizations outside the firm where the circle is located must, in large degree, be restricted.

CASE #27
Contacting Suppliers

When the electrical fabricators investigated the problem of fiberglass coverings for electrical cables (see Case #19), they uncovered a delicate problem in the quality circle process itself. It occurred as they investigated alternative products. Members wanted to know whether any other insulation material—without fiberglass—would do the job. To find out, they systematically contacted a number of companies by phone and by mail, asking for information. They also contacted the producer of the material they were using to see whether that company produced a different product that could be used.

Within a few days the circle leader received an urgent telephone call from the company's buyer who regularly dealt with the supplier. He was furious. The supplier had reacted with alarm to the telephone call from the quality circle members because the members had seemed to express disapproval with the product and wanted something else. But, asked the supplier, did they represent their company officially? Or had they accidentally leaked a major change? In short, he worried about his contract.

Worse still, the buyer knew nothing of the quality circle or the problem with the fiberglass. His lack of knowledge made him look foolish in front of one of his suppliers. He told the circle leader, in no uncertain terms, to contact a supplier only through him, the buyer.

The incident taught the circle and the program administrator a simple lesson about contacting "outside agencies," whether suppliers, customers, or government agencies: always go through proper channels.

As a result of that incident, the program administrator added a simple rule to the quality circle rule book: Whenever a circle must contact an outside agency—supplier, customer, union, or government—it must first contact the quality circle office and the office will determine how the contact is to be made.

The women in the electrical fabrication circle did not like the rule. Suspicious of their own organization, they felt that it would obscure the truth. They wanted the right to go directly to the source. Still, they understood the necessity of the rule and complied with it. Of course, they also understood their rights as citizens. The rule specifically restrained quality circle members of the company only from contacting suppliers—they could still talk to anyone they wished as private citizens after work.

• • •

Going through the quality circle office in order to contact outside organizations can be avoided in some cases. For example, if members of a circle normally make contact with outside organizations as part of their jobs, then the rule need not apply for those individuals and those contacts.

Reporting Circle Activities

Both managers and program administrators need a steady flow of information on the activities of circles to assure themselves that meetings are held and progress is made. Two reporting systems can meet this need: one produced by advisors who attend every meeting and one produced by circle secretaries and leaders. The former report goes to the program administrator. The latter goes up the line of management.

Advisors should report on every circle meeting in detail. The report can include a record of attendance, the stated purpose of the meeting, actual accomplishments, and a host of evaluations concerning leadership and participation, ending with an overall evaluation of both the meeting and the circle. Accumulated over time, this report becomes a history of the circle and provides concrete facts with which to identify patterns and build an objective understanding of what works and what does not work in an organization.

The circle report, prepared by the leader and the secretary, actually contains two reports. First, the secretary takes minutes, which include a record of attendance, a summary of the meeting discussion, a list of actions to be carried out, and the persons responsible for them. Second, the leader and the secretary prepare a monthly report for their circle's managers—general foreman and manager, for example. This includes the attendance record plus brief statements about the topic or problem that the circle is working on and a record of its accomplishments. The report should be signed by the advisor, the secretary, and the leader.

It is important that both these reporting systems exist. The quality circle office may be tempted to monopolize the flow of information on everyday circle activities in order to protect and sell the overall effort. If only the office reports on activities, however, it encourages managers to regard the circles as belonging to the office and not themselves or the members. Dual reporting diffuses this tendncy.

The dual system should interlock at some point in the hierarchy. If the circle sends its report to the general foreman and the manager, then the advisor's reports, summarized on a monthly basis, should go to these same managers. This provides corroboration and control for managers, as well as a way for them to evaluate and interpret the activities of their circles.

Presenting Proposals to Management

The management presentation highlights the entire quality circle process. The circle leader, and especially the advisor, must take great care to prepare members and make all the necessary arrangements. If successful, the presentation will have a tremendous motivational effect on the circle members. The stakes are high, however, and if they fail, the presentation can have a negative effect.

Fortunately, though it takes some time and a great deal of effort, anyone can prepare a successful management presentation, so long as certain key rules are observed.

Adequate preparation: A good proposal takes time to develop. Too many leaders and advisors accept quick solutions and simplistic, unrefined presentations. Always put quality before quantity or speed.

Adequate rehearsals: The success of management presentation depends heavily on the leader and advisor, who must direct presentation rehearsals and decide when members are ready to perform. They must never hurry the members or force them to present a proposal before they feel ready. Such caution can mean repeated delays, but taking extra time to be sure is worth it. Remember, speaking in public is very threatening for most people. They risk embarrassing themselves by inarticulateness, forgetting their part, dropping a pointer, or a million other small accidents. They, and the leader and advisor, want to perform in a manner that they can look back on with pride. If their performance embarrasses them, all motivational impact may be lost, even when management has approved their proposal.

To avoid embarrassment, circle members should divide the presentation into logical segments—introduction of members, statement of the topic or problem, analysis of its causes, presentation of a solution, justification of that solution, and a plan for implementation. Each member should present a specific part. Let members make viewgraphs and present their segment to the other members for a critique. When this process has produced a complete presentation, the members should present it to all the employees in their area who are not members of the circle for their review and comments. This should be followed with a dry run before someone who has never seen it before and knows nothing of the topic. The final step will show whether people who are totally unaware of the topic can follow the logic.

The advisor and leader should make sure that the proposal can be understood adequately from the viewgraphs themselves without benefit of spoken words. The final viewgraph of the presentation should be an "approval matrix" of some sort to serve as a guide to discussion after the presentation, encouraging managers to commit themselves to actions and deadlines, even if only for another meeting at a later date. Both these items are necessary, because the pitch will often serve as the major guide to implementation. If it cannot be understood in its written form, and if no names, commitments, and dates have been specified, implementation may never occur.

Choosing managers: Selecting the appropriate managers for a presentation requires serious forethought. If it is not done correctly, a number of problems can arise, some of which may injure the chances of success for a proposal and damage a quality circle effort.

First, the circle may invite the wrong managers, or may invite all the necessary managers except the crucial one. This kind of mistake creates an air of incompetence at worst, a lack of professionalism at best. Moreover, it results in a meeting that annoys or angers managers and embarrasses members.

Second, the circle may bypass a manager—purposefully or inadvertently—and present the proposal to his boss. Most circles naturally attempt this "end-run" play. They see immediate management as the obstacle to positive change, often as the enemy, and feel that they can win their case if they can just get their message to upper management. This unnecessarily puts middle managers on the spot, embarrassing them to such an extent that they become lifelong enemies of quality circles (see Case #3).

To avoid the unfortunate by-product of end-runs, the leader and advisor of every circle should follow these steps to determine the highest level to which a proposal should be taken: Determine what departments would be needed for implementation. Estimate the level of authority in each department that is needed to evaluate and implement a proposal and move one level above them to their common boss. In no case, however, should a pitch go higher than the *lowest* level necessary for implementation.

Move up the chain of command in stages. Following the steps just outlined, the circle should make a "middle management" presentation first, to all foremen, general foremen, and managers who would be affected by the proposal. This meeting should also include every specialist and manager who helped the circle prepare the proposal so that they have an opportunity to make a final comment, *pro* or *con*. The members should also ask those present to indicate who should be invited to the "upper management" presentation. This final meeting should, of course, include all the people whose knowledge and advice are pertinent to the decision, most of them having already seen the pitch in the middle management presentation.

This staged approach to presentation serves a number of purposes: It reduces the risk of end-runs. It involves the widest possible net of managers in the solution, something that is positive and beneficial to implementation. It exposes and educates the widest number of managers to the quality circle process in action. And, most of all, it leads to valid decisions on projects that will stand up over time and have a high probability of quick implementation.

In planning presentations, the leader and advisor should not be miserly with invitations. For all the reasons just enumerated, the more people present, the better the results for the specific circle and the quality circle process and the organization as a whole. Members and leaders tend to be timid. They should not be. Broadcast even the simplest proposal far and wide.

Telephone those who are invited to find out whether they can attend at a designated time. Later, remind them by formal memorandum and a follow-up telephone call on the day of the pitch.

Even though a pitch needs to go to only middle management, invite upper management as guests. This lets them know what is happening, even if they do not attend, and it lets the middle managers, who otherwise might take less heed, know that the boss might attend.

As a special task, prepare key managers for the presentation. Few managers, regardless of the scope and detail of a presentation, are willing to make a decision on the spot. To ask them to do so risks the easiest responses—either a flat "No" or "Give us a week or two to look it over in more detail." To avoid this, and as a necessary courtesy, sit down with key decision makers in the days prior to the pitch and give them a sneak preview.

CASE #28
The Director Redeems Himself

A year after its difficult and unsuccessful interaction with the tool fabrication quality circle (see Case #3), the director of manufacturing was about to receive another proposal from one of his shops. By this time, however, circle members throughout the facility, circle advisors, and managers had all learned a great deal about how to interact with each other before, during, and after presentations.

The director had participated in a five-hour seminar on quality circles and the role of the manager. Monthly reports had passed up the chain of command to his managers, and they, in turn, had mentioned current projects during his regular staff meetings. He knew what was coming and he knew how to deal with it.

The most important thing was that the advisor scheduled a meeting with the director one day before the management presentation and walked him through a copy of the circle's proposal. The director listened attentively, but was not impressed. It seemed to him that, although the problem was serious, the proposed solution looked too expensive.

The circle, a mechanical assembly circle (see Case #1) that had already given a successful presentation and felt confident of its abilities, proposed a new workstand for a relatively minor job. They knew that, on its own merit, their solution might not justify its expense, though the problem it was intended to solve was real enough.

The circle presented their suggestion to middle management first. They invited their foreman, their general foreman, a representative from tool design who had worked with them over the last few months, and a planner. The general foreman expressed the greatest skepticism. He felt that the proposal was mechanically sound and that it would solve a real problem that had plagued them for years, but he could not justify the cost—roughly $25,000. During the discussion, however, the planner revealed that a new stand was already in the long-range budget. It had been intended to support welders but, with minor additions, would also serve the needs of the mechanical assemblers. Given that fact, they could justify the cost since, in essence, the stand was already approved. The circle was elated. The general foreman, too, saw no problem with the proposal.

When the advisor had finished explaining the proposal, the director insisted on walking to the floor to see the problem firsthand. There, looking at the present working arrangements—which included a wooden stepladder and an unsteady lift—he became convinced of the urgency of the problem, but he remained unconvinced about the solution. He was, he said, working under a very tight budget. The advisor left it at that. He had fulfilled his obligation to inform the director of the content of the proposal. However, when he returned to his office, he called the manager of tool design and explained that the director seemed unaware of the long-term plan to build another workstand. The manager said he would talk to the director before the pitch.

Although the advisor did not learn of it until after the presentation, the manager spent an hour that afternoon with the director going over the long-range plan and exploring all alternatives and options. Eventually, they convinced each other that, not only was the stand going to be built, but that the circle's proposal made good sense and should be implemented.

When the presentation finally took place, it occurred without a hitch. The members sounded articulate and concise. When they finished, the director complimented them on their work and led other managers in an orderly discussion of the *pros* and *cons* of the proposal. They agreed to build the workstand and to include the additions proposed by the quality circle.

Following Up on Proposals

In the glow of a successful management presentation, members, leaders, advisor, and invited managers often forget a key element. They forget to state clearly who bears responsibility for taking what action and when. As a consequence, the project is implemented incorrectly, is implemented very slowly, or is not implemented at all.

This collapse of the quality circle process at the most crucial moment—the handing of responsibility from circle members to the organization—can destroy a quality circle effort.

A previous section outlined a system by which an agency within the organization tracks projects to see to it that they are implemented. But the circle must also track a project to make sure that all is being done correctly and expeditiously from its viewpoint. A few simple devices aid in this process.

Approval matrix: Every presentation should contain an approval matrix which designates actions to be taken, costs, agencies responsible, individuals who accept the responsibilities, telephone numbers, dates when they expect to complete the action, interim dates they will communicate back to the circle, and general comments. As an actual element in the presentation, this matrix forces managers and the circle members to commit themselves during the presentation.

Project reporting: Using the approval matrix as a guide, a circle leader and advisor should fill out a project report and pass it to the agency in the organization that tracks quality circle projects. This report might include all the information in the approval matrix plus a clear statement of the project, a list of the circle members, the date of the presentation, and a complete copy of the pitch. In the hands of the tracking agency, this document becomes the official "folder," or record, of the project and is closed only when the project has been completed to everyone's satisfaction.

Bird-dogging: None of these devices, however, can substitute for tracking the project yourself. The circle members must continually monitor what occurs. They can call the individuals who took responsibility for following up by inviting them to the circle meeting to explain what they have done. If they find that someone has dropped the ball, the circle can encourage him to fulfill his assignment, go to his boss to complain, go to someone else, embarrass him, or employ any other tactic that seems advisable. What they cannot and must not do is hand over the project to management and then drop it. They must stay with it to completion.

Measuring success: One way to see that people stick with a project is to measure its impact on the original problem. Members can maintain a control chart on the defects the circle intends to control. If the number of defects has declined, when their solution is implemented, they know they have succeeded. They can continue to maintain the control chart to assure themselves that the problem stays solved, or to give them early warning of new problems.

CASE #29
Case #28 Continued

Once the director and managers had completed their discussion of the project, they filled in the blanks on the approval matrix. There was only one item, the new stand. The tool design manager agreed to send his designer to the next meeting with rough drawings of the stand. The members would then be able to discuss with the designer exactly what they needed, and he would continue to meet with them on a regular basis until the drawings were complete. Once the drawings were finished, the project would move into tool fabrication, final inspection, and then to the manufacturing area.

At this point responsibility for the project passed to the managers and technical specialists, who had agreed to take certain actions by signing the approval matrix. To ensure that they fulfilled their promises, the advisor and the leader filled out a project report—containing the proposal and the approval matrix—and sent it to the designated officer in the office of planning and control for the entire organization. It was his responsibility to push the project along by periodically telephoning managers and technical specialists to remind them of their obligations.

In the meantime, the circle members tracked the progress of their proposal themselves. They called the tool design area regularly. They called the tool fabrication area, and they contacted circle members in the tool fabrication shop and asked them to watch for the project to make sure that it did not become buried or lost or—worse still—constructed incorrectly.

Evaluating Circle Growth and Development

Every circle has its own style and pace, but despite this diversity, certain patterns of growth or development always take shape. When they do not appear, something is amiss. Find out what's wrong and correct it.

Attendance: Attendance measures a circle's health. Advisors and program administrators and managers should all watch it closely. If it begins to decline, take note and keep a worried eye on the circle. If it continues to decline, become alarmed and begin to talk to each of the members to find out why they are not attending the meetings. There is always a reason why people do not attend, and often it is not the first reason given.

Presentations: Most circles take between six and nine months to make their first management presentation. This may seem like a long time, but remember, they have only one hour per week to meet and work on their project. Six to nine months represents only 26 to 39 hours of meeting time. Training occupies the first four or five sessions, and after that members need time to settle into a comfortable and smoothly functioning work group. The actual process of choosing a problem, analyzing its causes, and producing a solution takes time to do correctly. Meticulous, systematic methodology produces good results; quick "suggestions" do not. And preparation for a management presentation requires a great deal of time, especially for the first one. Most members are not accustomed to public speaking and require careful guidance and rehearsal.

Once they have completed their first presentation, circles average two to three presentations each year. Some may exceed this pace, of course, and some may fall short, but unfortunately, for some reason managers and even some program administrators feel that circles should be "more productive." They prod circle members to put out more solutions, and in so doing they turn members off. Too much pushing poisons the atmosphere, and the program suffers. Members must be left to choose their projects and set their own pace. Managers, program administrators, and advisors need to be patient.

Disbanding a Circle

Sooner or later, every quality circle effort runs out of steam and the circle "dies." Administrators, advisors, and managers should expect and prepare for this eventuality. It happens, but it is not necessarily a disaster.

If attendance declines and the circle appears to be ineffectual, find out why. If you can determine the cause and correct it, so much the better. If not, establish a procedure for shutting down the circle without conveying a sense of failure.

Sometimes the explanation is simple. The tool fabrication circle described in Case #3 "died" primarily because of internal disagreement over the role of supervision, but also because the circle's third proposal was mishandled. Another, less clear-cut example follows.

CASE #30
Inactive

Quality inspectors formed the first circle at this facility. The managers supported the circle, which met regularly without interference. Composed of the supervisor and all employees in his department, it fit the ideal model. When training was complete, the circle tried to choose a problem to solve. It was not easy. People seemed unable to list problems affecting their area, yet they insisted that their area had problems.

The ineffectiveness of the circle alarmed the advisor, who searched in vain for a specific "external" cause. Finding none, the advisor concluded that the members themselves were not up to the task. The leader, in particular, could not handle the simplest organizational task, and no other member came forth to fill the void. One elderly gentleman regularly fell asleep. Another man in his late twenties seemed always to be "stoned." He habitually made comments out of context. A middle-aged woman sat in hostile silence. The other members were full of good intentions, but they could never focus on an issue and stick with it.

Within a few weeks, attendance began to drop. The first to stay away was the supervisor-leader. The meetings embarrassed him by revealing his complete lack of leadership talent. Then the hostile middle-aged woman ceased to come. She felt, as she expressed it, that the whole thing was a waste of time. The old man quit too. Finally, the four other members had to admit that there was little reason to continue. They declared the circle "inactive."

More than a year later, the supervisor and many of the

original members had changed departments. New employees and an aggressive supervisor asked the office to help them to reactivate and retrain the circle. It now functions smoothly.

• • •

The first lesson in dealing with "failed" circles is to stop defining them as "failed." As in the example, "inactive" more accurately describes the condition. Every shop or office has the potential for a circle, and even those that have stopped meeting can, and probably will, "reactivate" one year, two years, or even five years hence. In many instances, a circle may find it useful to declare itself inactive for a specified period of time. For example, if a work crew is broken up and reassigned to other shops, members can declare their circle inactive until they are reassembled as a work crew.

In every case, whatever the motivation or cause, the remaining members, not the office, should declare the circle inactive. They chose to form a circle. It was their circle. They should formally disband it.

Codifying the Rules

The rules for setting up and operating quality circles should be established before the first steps are taken. This will help you avoid many problems. In print and available to all, the rules will underwrite the administrator's ability to enforce them and ensure control of the program.

Eight general categories of rules need to be set forth:

• Forming a circle
• Scheduling circle meetings
• Leading circle meetings

- Choosing problems and projects
- Requesting information from technical specialists and outside agencies
- Reporting to management
- Giving management presentations
- Following up on projects

CASE #31
Written Rules

As the production welders (Case #10) worked on their project to decrease the time spent testing welder certification test panels, they stumbled onto a basic problem. In order to inspect panels, test them, cut them, deburr them, test them again, and so on, the panels had to be moved from shop to shop. Each move required another shop's intervention, a folder, and a computer input. The circle's investigation showed that all this moving from place to place, with its associated documentation, was the root of the problem.

The solution? The quality circle simply proposed that one man, located in the quality laboratory, would complete all steps. Panels would not move from one shop to another, folders would not be necessary, and no one would have to make a computer input. Simple enough, but one obstacle blocked their plan: The laboratory was a nonunion shop, and the movement of the various processes to a specific location constituted "taking work" from union employees.

All the production welders, to whom the problem was a matter of communication, were union members. They immediately contacted the union agent and invited him to their next meeting. Their advisor was aware that dealing with job classifications was against the rules of the quality circle process in his organization, but he was slow to realize exactly what had happened. To him, the rule against dealing with job classifications referred to the original choice of a problem, not the proposed solution. The circle seemed to be following a logical course of action, one that involved little danger and good possibility of success.

When the meeting took place, he quickly realized his mistake. Word had gotten to the personnel department that a circle planned to meet with a union representative and they rushed a company representative to the session also. There in the room were both sides, as though they were negotiating.

The union agent thought the proposal was a good one, but recognized that it caused problems in other shops where people would resent the loss of work. Though the circle members questioned him at length, he remained noncommittal. He would not say one way or another what the union's position would be. He implied that the union would "react" to the company's position when and if the company accepted the proposal. The representative from personnel expressed even more caution. He merely observed without comment.

With his realization that the circle had backed into a real problem and had, in fact, violated two rules—dealing with job classifications and talking to the union or other outside agency—the advisor quickly moved to avert a crisis. He explained the situation to the leader and together at the next regular meeting they explained that the circle had inadvertently gotten itself into a tight spot. He proposed that they cease conversations with the union and present the entire matter to management for decision and action. If management found the circle's proposal a good one, management would create the new job and would deal with the union through the usual channels. In effect, he told the circle members that they had taken the project as far as they could and should now turn it over to management. Fortunately, all circle members had received extensive training, which included a review of the rules of quality circle activities. In fact, everyone had a small booklet containing all the rules. As a result, they accepted the advice without question. They understood that there had been a violation of the rules, and they recognized the danger that certain rules were created to avoid. If circles began to "negotiate" with either the company or the union on matters traditionally handled by normal procedures of the union and the company, they would subvert the entire process of company-union problem solving and conflict resolution. They saw that some things were best handled by the union, while others could be handled by circles.

Summary

You should move cautiously and methodically through the steps just described. As with most important undertakings, the probability of success is directly proportional to the amount of thoughtful preparation. Thus, begin your effort with extensive investigation of the quality circle process in other organizations, on your own and through consultants. Obtain management understanding and approval. Involve the union. Develop sponsorship within the organization, set up an office, and hire a staff.

Next, spend as much time as necessary to develop a strategy and the training courses to support it. At the same time, prepare the organization by setting up one system to implement circle proposals and another system to measure the results of quality circle participation. Evaluate the incentive structure of your organization to be sure that it promotes, rather than hinders, participation in quality circles. Determine how your circle will acquire technical support. Finally, begin to write out the working details—the rules—of the quality circle process.

Only after all this is accomplished should you begin forming and training circles. Diagrams 15 and 16 chart average progress.

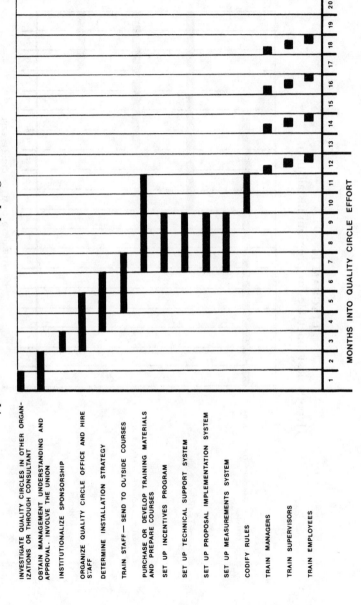

DIAGRAM 15

Hypothetical timetable for start-up program.

DIAGRAM 16

Hypothetical timetable for program installation.

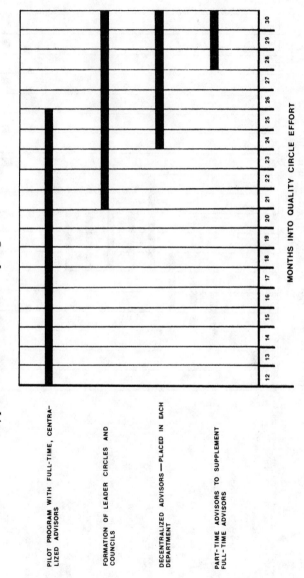

PART THREE
Interpreting the Quality Circle Process

9

A Political Process

What does a fully developed quality circle process do to an organization that eventually results in improved employee performance? Obviously, it changes it. But what does it change? And how should we conceive of this change?

There is only one answer that adequately explains the magnitude of the positive results. *The quality circle process changes the power relations between upper management, middle management, supervision, and employees.* To understand what is going on, *we must view the organization as a political system and the quality circle process as a political process.*

A Political System

Every organization has a goal, whether it is to produce a product or provide a service. Every organization must attain this goal within certain economic constraints—the necessity of making a profit or staying within a prescribed budget. To meet its goal, within its economic constraints, an organization divides itself into parts or subgroups, each with its separate but essential function. These subgroups interact as a system, affecting each other through various processes. Central among these processes are all forms of decision making.

Every formal organization has certain decision-making

centers or arenas. These are usually individuals (such as the plant manager) or committees (such as a weekly staff meeting to review the production schedule). Into these arenas, the subgroups, usually through representatives, present their inputs. These inputs are usually relevant information, new proposals, or demands or requests that reflect the interests of the subgroup—money to operate, changes in the rules of the organization, changes in schedules, and so on. Decision makers, often including the very people making the requests, consider the inputs and, in the interest of the organization as a whole, make a decision. Once decided, the result—simple information, a new procedure, a new budget, schedule changes, rule changes, and so on—is transmitted to all the subgroups, especially the ones that must take action on the decision. The process, then, is one in which input moves in from the subgroups to decision-making arenas, and decisions move out to the subgroups.

This simple model excludes all personal career interests. They affect the process, but they are not essential for understanding it. What I am talking about is the obvious, daily stuff of organization life. Perhaps it can most clearly be demonstrated by example. Let us say that the quality control director wants more funds to hire more inspectors to maintain product quality. The manufacturing director, in direct conflict, may want the inspection rules lightened so that the inspectors will not constantly bring production to a halt over every minor discrepancy. The finance director may wish to cut labor expenses and increase plant productivity to improve profits, while the marketing director maintains that they must produce higher-quality products if they are going to remain competitive. For the organization to function, all these people must meet in a decision-making arena so that they can present their views and arrive at a policy decision which they can live with. Once the decision is made, they must assign responsibilities for carrying out any actions entailed.

Unfortunately, most organizations leave most of their employees out of this process. The higher-ranked minority—management—excludes the lower-ranked majority—employees—from decision-making arenas. They assume that the interests of employees are in conflict with the goals of the organization. They reject the input of employees, make decisions without it, and force the decisions on employees without their consent.

Most organizations operate in this dictatorial fashion, some benevolent, some rather harsh. Like dictatorships everywhere, the system may survive, but it is very inefficient. Often a decision made without the participation of those who must put it into effect is unrealistic, and as a result when it reaches the bottom level as an order, people who deal with the facts find they must circumvent it if the task is to be accomplished. Disenfranchised employees—noncitizens of the organization—quickly become lethargically indifferent at best, actively hostile at worst. Some attack the organization by sabotage, others quit, fleeing like refugees to another organization in hopes of a better deal. Poor decisions, unproductive indifference, purposeful sabotage, high turnover, and, ultimately, the cost of enforcing compliance to the system all contribute to the inefficiency. Worst of all, the system disallows the potential contributions of most of the people within it.

In such organizations, the quality circle process amounts to nothing less than *political reform*. It enfranchises employees by allowing them to participate directly in the decision-making process. It makes them contributing citizens of the organization. Thus, when the mechanical assembly quality circle (Case #1) proposed and got a new tool, the major objective may have been to improve the quality of their work—solve a technical production problem—but the process was preeminently political. They had to articulate their interest, their need: a better tool. They had to develop an argument for the new tool that would persuade the people with the power of decision, management, to build and install it. Then they had to gain access to the centers of decision making and lobby for their interest. The process is not very different from the political process at the local, state, or national level.

Power Within the Organization

Political reform, even the very limited reforms of quality circles, means changing the distribution and nature of power within an organization. Simply put, the quality circle process gives employees limited power that they did not formerly have by letting them into the decision-making process. At the same time, it weakens managers and supervisors by breaking their monopoly of communications between employees and upper managers and support specialists. To understand how this occurs, we must first develop a simple model and a set of terms.

An organization is, first of all, a group of *actors.* In a state of anarchy, in the absence of organization, these actors could interact in an infinite and unpredictable number of ways, each pursuing private goals. A formal organization, like any social system, attains a high degree of order by restricting the social relations of its actors to specific *roles*—clusters of prescribed behaviors that an actor is expected to exhibit toward other actors in a given context. Prescribed behaviors are best thought of as *rules.* In formal organizations, there are three significant kinds of rules: moral principles, jural rules, and technical facts.*

* Ralph W. Nicholas, "Rules, Resources and Political Activity," in *Local-Level Politics: Social and Cultural Perspectives,* Marc J. Swartz, ed. Chicago: Aldine Publishing Company, 1968, pp. 302–307.

Moral principles: Moral principles do not come to mind when we think of formal organizations, yet they are clearly present. They are the tacit definitions of what the organization and the actors within it should value and strive for. They are what one "should" or "ought" to do. They are invoked in the widest contexts to regulate behavior. *Cost effectiveness* and *productivity,* for example, are moral principles common to industrial organizations. They are frequently invoked to justify decisions and influence behavior. *Product quality* and *employee participation* might also serve as moral principles in the same sense.

Jural rules: These are the organization's procedures and conventions, written or remembered, with which everyone is expected to comply. Violators can expect to be punished. In a formal organization, for example, most employees must arrive at work before a certain time and leave after a certain time. While on the job, they must engage in what the organization defines as productive work, with the exception of authorized breaks for lunch and rest. Violation of these rules will lead to punishment ranging from a warning to dismissal.

Technical facts: Statements of what is "necessary" constitute technical facts in an organization's system of rules. They regulate behavior by their presence or absence. For example, an employee must have access to relevant information and must possess the necessary organizational skills to participate in certain decision-making processes. Without these things he cannot act effectively and will be disregarded.

Formal organizations also restrict the behavior of actors by limiting the amount of control they have over resources, both material and human.

Material resources are economic factors—money, materials, and machines. In an organization, we speak of "control" over these resources, rather than ownership. The control an actor has over any part of the material resources available depends, first, on his or her position within the hierarchy and second, on the jural rules associated with that position.

The control an actor has over *human resources*—the labor and actions of others—is regulated in the same way.

Quality Circles and Power

In the game of organizational politics, management has all the power. It controls all the resources and makes the rules. Without quality circles, it structures the rules to keep employees out of the decision-making process altogether. That, they say, is management's prerogative. With quality circles, management changes the rules slightly to grant employees just enough power to allow them to participate in the decision-making process on subjects that relate directly to their immediate work.

Without quality circles: In the absence of quality circles, the average employee at the bottom of the hierarchy has little or no ability to influence decisions that bear on his work and his work area. He is powerless and dependent. He has no control over material resources—money, machinery, and materials—which belong to the organization and are controlled by management, and he has no control over human resources. He does not supervise those other employees he can call on to do work for him. Most important, his only resources—his native intelligence and his accumulated knowledge and skill—remain latent because the organization allows him no opportunity to mobilize them.

Those resources might serve the interests of both himself and the organization, but they remain unused because of a series of rules. First, there is the obvious fact that he has no time or space in which to develop and articulate ideas about his work and work area, and even if he could, he lacks the training and support necessary to present his ideas in a form that the organization can understand.

Second, jural rules enforce these facts. The organization defines "work." It says when, where, how, and what will be done. It places an enforcer, the supervisor, in the shop to ensure that work is carried out as defined. Any violation of the rules of when, where, how, and what brings immediate rebuke. Never does the organization provide the time, space, and freedom from enforcement so that the employee can make his input to the definition. Moreover, it prevents, not so much by commission as by omission, the employee from gaining access to decision-making arenas in which the when, where, how, and what of every job are decided. It withholds training in basic management skills such as simple problem solving, planning procedures, and presentation techniques. It offers no accepted, structured means for employees to communicate personally with decision makers. At best, if they have an idea, they can submit it through a suggestion system or pass it on to their supervisor.

This entire system is underwritten by a moral principle. Most managers, and many employees as well, adhere to the belief set forth by Frederick W. Taylor in the very early part of this century that there should be total division of labor between those who think and those who do. They use this principle to exclude employees from decision making and to restrict their time, space, and knowledge. They try to make them an extension, if not an equivalent, of a machine. Only then, they believe, can they maximize productivity.

With quality circles: By installing quality circles, management grants the average employee the opportunity to participate directly in decisions that affect his work and workplace. This change is achieved by altering slightly some of the rules of the political system of the organization.

First, management changes key technical facts. It gives employees the time—usually one hour each week—and the place—usually a room separated from the work area—to meet and discuss work-related subjects. It provides special training in techniques for identifying and solving problems that are inhibiting greater productivity and higher quality. And it provides training and support in the process of communicating proposals to management.

Second, it changes the jural rules that enforce the technical facts. It redefines work to include the discussion and thought that goes on in a quality circle meeting. It grants the time and space necessary for the meetings. During the meetings it assures freedom from enforcement of the organization's standard definition of work and, in its place, gives the circle members the right to consider whatever topics they wish, provided they relate to their work. Above all, it sets up the jural rules which allow employees, as circle members, access to decision-making arenas.

Ultimately, the formation of quality circles requires that the moral principles supporting sharp division of labor be amended to include participation by all employees in the decision-making process under the rules of the quality circle process. This right to participate is returned to the employee in an institutionalized process that benefits the organization as well as the employee.

The Structural Limitations of Power

Under the standard system, where quality circles do not exist, the basic management strategy for enforcing its principles of work is to control employees by dealing with them strictly as individuals. Work itself is typically divided and subdivided into individual tasks. Pay is made to individuals. All recognition, awards, and advancement are for individual achievement. It is rare indeed that recognition is given to group achievement. Diagram 17 illustrates this principle.

This strategy is obviously aimed at maintaining absolute control over employees. At all costs, employees must not gain power through unified action, because the only way to control them is to set all employees in competition with each other. Group activities instill nervous concern in management, which regards joint action as hostile and threatening.

The simple changes in the rules to permit quality circles to exist bring the power and right to form a group. This very permission, by legitimizing group activity, alters its nature. Instead of being hostile, in defiance of the company, it is cooperative. But the group formed does not include *all* employees of a certain labor grade. Rather, it is a small group of employees from a single shop or office. As a result of its small size and specific shop focus, as well as the explicit rules of the quality circle process, the "interests" that its members can articulate are limited to their immediate work—such things as improved tools, procedural changes, product innovations, safety improvements, and production and cost-saving shortcuts. They do not involve more general, organizationwide issues such as wages and salaries. Diagram 18 shows these relationships.

With quality circles, the strategy is still divide and control, but its application is more subtle and sophisticated. We divide by small groups rather than by individuals. We encourage competition between these groups and cooperation within them rather than competition between individuals. Since the groups are formed around areas congruent with the effective functioning of the organization,

DIAGRAM 17
Old structure.

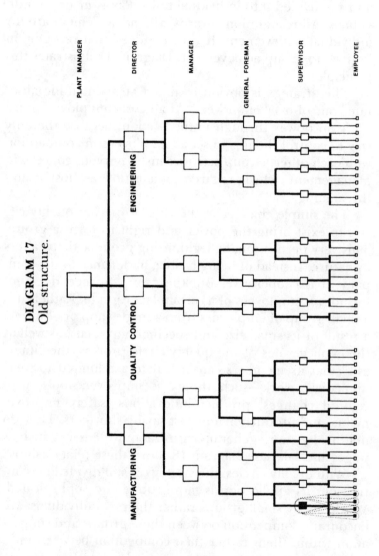

DIAGRAM 18
New structure.

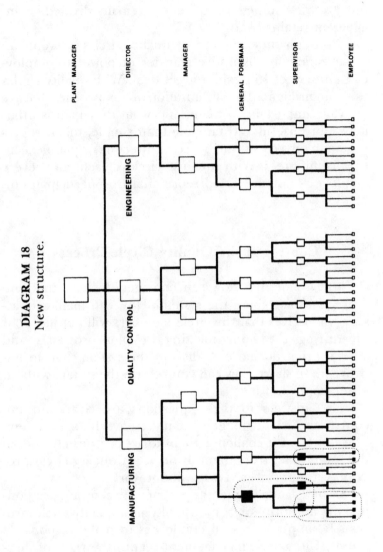

their cooperation is beneficial to the organization. Since the groups compete and, hence, remain divided, management retains control.

Although the structure of quality circles prevents an organizationally disruptive transfer of power to employees, employees still gain a great deal. With quality circles they can influence the organization on many issues that are critically important to them, and what they gain is infinitely more useful and tangible than simple, token representation on a corporate board of directors or plant executive committee. With quality circles, each and every employee—not an elected representative—participates directly.

Control of the Quality Circle Process

Reform is fine, but how can managers be sure that employees do not abuse the system? How can managers assure themselves that the circle members will not just goof off during the hour meeting or plot proposals and schemes that do more to disrupt the system than to improve it? In short, how can you reform the system without losing control of it?

The answers to these questions are clear and unequivocal. First, management must have faith in its employees. It must challenge them to act responsibly and, at the same time, trust them to do so. A quality circle program without sincere trust will not work.

Second, management does not give away decision-making authority or responsibility in a quality circle process. It simply allows all employees to make responsible inputs. Ultimately, management retains the right of decision through the mechanism of the management presentation.

Third, management must not install a quality circle process without careful preparation. This procedure can be summarized:

1. Form and locate an office within the organization to promote quality circles.
2. Develop a strategy of implementation that allows the office to maintain adequate control of the installation process.
3. Prepare a training program for all members of the organization.
4. Formulate clear-cut guidelines, even rules, about the operation of quality circles.
5. Prepare the organization to provide incentives and technical expertise, implement circle proposals, and measure the impact of the quality circle effort.

Basically, the best method of control is a cautious, unhurried, thoughtful, realistic process of installation that is based on a clear image of the long-term objective and which recognizes the problem and pitfalls that can undermine its attainment.

Index

absenteeism, quality circles as reducing, 11
abuse of quality circles, avoiding,
188–189
see also control(s)
accessibility, importance of, 116–
119, 151–155
accidents, quality circles as reducing, 11, 116
accomplishments
individual *vs.* group, 185–188
recording of, 156
see also evaluation
actors, organizations as composed
of, 180–182
administrator, program
as quality circle position, 58,
59–61
relationship of advisor to,
85–95, 99
advancement, career, as incentive,
25, 112
advisors
as consultants, 96–98
full-time, 84–91
part-time, 84, 91–96
problems related to, 34, 37–40,
116–119
proposal presentations as responsibility of, 157–165
relationship of supervisors to,
see supervisors
role of, in quality circles, 4, 16,
58, 60–61
training of, *see* training
Toyota Auto Body's use of, 20,
24
advisory techniques, as area of
special training, 101–102
agencies, government, as information source, 154

American Society for Quality
Control, as information
source, 47
analysis
cause-and-effect, 4, 105
Pareto, 4, 23, 105
approval, quality circle
importance of, from top management, 42–43
winning of, 51–52
see also installation, quality circle
approval matrix, as means of
follow-up, 163
arena, as decision-making center,
177–178
employee's access to, 184
association circles, professional,
138–141
attendance, meeting
as element of circle report,
155–156
as growth evaluation tool, 165
see also participation
attitude, employee, 116
attitude survey
as method of evaluation, 26,
131
use of, by advisor, 85
attrition, quality circles as reducing, 11, 116
authoritarian leadership
advisor for, 99
teaching of, 105
authority
end-runs and, 158–160
threatening of, 67, 74, 79, 82
see also leadership

behavioral approach to training,
102

bird-dogging, as means of
follow-up, 163–164
bonus, as incentive, 21, 25, 111–
112
bottom-up strategy, 65–72
middle-down strategy and,
72–84
brainstorming, as area of special
training, 4, 105
bulletins, use of, for recognition,
110

cancellation, meeting, 147–149
career development, as incentive
for quality circle participation, 25, 112
cause-and-effect analysis, as area
of special training, 4, 105
central organizing unit, 55–64
codification, rule, 168–171
cognitive approach to training,
102
commitment
importance of, 41
as responsibility of top management, 26
winning, from top manage-
ment, 51–52
committees
steering, 52–55, 121
see also councils
competition, as incentive for quality circle participation, 20, 25,
110–111
conferences, as motivating factor,
111
consultants
advisors as, 96–98
use of, in quality circles, 46–47,
53
see also specialists
contracts, union, 43–44
control(s)
limiting resources as method of,
181, 182
maintaining, 187–189
Toyota Auto Body's use of,
25–27
control chart, as means of follow-
up, 164

cost effectiveness, as moral principle, 181
conventions, organizational,
180–181
councils
leader, 98–99, 123
see also committees; group(s)

decision making
employees' roles in, 179–180,
182–184
as essential business function,
177–179
see also problem solving
decision-making arena, 177–178,
184
dedication
importance of, 41
as responsibility of top management, 26
winning, from top manage-
ment, 51–52
development, career, 25, 112
dictatorial organization, 179
direct financial incentives, 111–
112
disbanding of quality circles,
166–168
dismissal, as resulting from jural
rule violation, 181
divisional steering committee,
54–55
division of labor, 183
dual reporting, 155–156

education
steering committee's role in, 53
see also training
empire building, 89, 90–91, 93
employees
absenteeism of, 11
accomplishments of, 185–188
attitude of, 116
career development of, 25, 112
decision making by, 179–189
evaluation of, *see* evaluation
incentives for, *see* incentives
participation in quality circles
by, *see* participation
power relations of, 177

employees (*continued*)
  presentations by, 156–165
  punishment of, 181
  recognition of, 110–111
  recruiting, 134–135
  role of, in quality circles, *see* quality circles
  as selecting projects, 4, 150–151, 166
  selling quality circle idea to, 72
  training of, *see* training
end-runs, 160
enforcer, supervisor as, 183
evaluation
  areas of, 124–131
  failure of, as pitfall, 32
  growth, attendance as tool for, 165
  as quality control process, 14, 17, 105
  reporting system for, 155–156
  by Toyota Auto Body, 23–24, 25–26
executives, *see* management
executive steering committee, 53–54
explanation of quality circle
  as important step in installing, 47–49, 99
  see also installation, quality circle
external information, 151, 153–155
extrinsic motives, 109
  see also incentives

failure
  of quality circle, 160–168
  of proposal implementation, 32, 119–123
  of quality circle evaluation, 32
fear
  as basis for quality circle resistance, 82
  use of training to avoid, 106
financial incentives, *see* money
flexibility, importance of, 135
flow charts, as area of special training, 4, 23, 105
follow up, proposal, 162–165

full-time advisors, 84–91, 95
  as consultants, 96–99
  see also advisors

General Dynamics, 12–13
goals, *see* objectives
government agencies, as information source, 154
grievances, quality circle as reducing, 11, 116
group(s)
  role of, in quality circles, 3–4, 15–17
  study, 108
  sub, 177–178
  target, *see* target groups
  training of, *see* training
  see also meetings, quality circle
group achievements *vs.* individual achievements, 185–188
growth
  career, 25, 112
  circle, evaluating, 165–166

histograms, as area of special training, 23, 105
Honeywell, 11
human resources, control over, 181–182

identification, problem, 14, 17, 105
implementation, proposal
  failure of, as pitfall, 32
  follow-up for, 119–123
  problems of, in interorganizational circles, 147
  as quality circle process, 14, 17, 105
  role of steering committee in, 54
  see also presentations
inactivity, circle, 168
incentives
  career development, 112
  financial, 111–112
  quality circle start-up, 20–21, 25–26, 109–110
  recognition as, 110–111
  structuring, 113–116

indirect financial incentives,
111–112
individual achievement *vs.* group
achievement, 185–188
information, requesting, 151–155
installation, quality circle
advisors for, *see* advisors
approval for, 41–43, 51–52
commitment towards, 51–52
disbanding, 166–168
employees' role in, *see* employees
explaining, 47–51
incentives for, 20–21, 25–26,
109–116
management's role in, *see* management
participation in, *see* participation, quality circle
problems to avoid during,
31–47
proposals for, *see* implementation, proposal
of quality circle office, *see* office,
quality circle
responsibility for, 55–56
results of, *see* evaluation
sponsoring, 52–55
strategies for, 66
structure of, 14–17, 135–147
timetable for, 174
training for, *see* training
union involvement in, 43–45,
72, 150–151, 154, 171
see also quality circles
instruction, *see* training
integrated circle, as variation of
quality circle, 141–144
International Association of Quality Circles
as information source, 47, 111
purchasing of training tools
from, 103
interorganizational circle, as variation of quality circle, 144–147
intrinsic motives, 109
see also incentives

Japanese quality circles
general statistics on, 18–19

Toyota Auto Body as example
of, 19–26
Japanese Union of Scientists and
Engineers, 20, 111
jural rules, 180–181
effects of, on employees, 183
quality circles as changing,
184

labor, division of, 183
leader, quality circle, 3–4, 15, 24
problems related to, 149–150
relationship of advisor to, 86,
96–99
responsibility of, 157–165
supervisor as, 80–84
training for, *see* training
see also leadership
leader circles, 98–99, 123
see also quality circles
leader councils, 98–99, 123
leadership
authoritarian, 99, 105
dictatorial, 179
end-runs and, 158–160
participative, 99, 105
threatening of, 67, 74, 79, 82,
187–188
learning, *see* training
lectures, as training tool, 102
limitations of power, 184–188
see also control(s)
location of quality circle meeting,
4
see also office, quality circle
loyality
quality circle as increasing, 11
see also commitment

management
approval of quality circles by,
42–43, 51–52
authoritarian, 99, 105
commitment of, 51–52
as control factor, 25
dictatorial, 179
integrated circles as affecting,
144
misunderstanding of quality
circles by, 31

management (*continued*)
   ownership of quality circle by,
      see ownership
   participative, 99, 105
   power relations within, 177–
      189
   proposal implementation and,
      119–123, 156–166
   role of, in organization, *see* or-
      ganization
   training of, *see* training
Martin Marietta Corporation, 12,
   126
material resources, control over,
   181–182
matrix, approval, as means of
   follow-up, 163
meetings, quality circle
   attendance at, 155–156
   consultants for, 46–47, 53
   decision making within, 4,
      179–180, 182–184
   employees' roles in, *see* employ-
      ees
   general information on, 3–4
   leaders for, *see* leader, quality
      circle
   leading, 149–150
   management's role in, *see* man-
      agement
   office for, *see* office, quality cir-
      cle
   participation at, *see* participa-
      tion
   projects for, 4, 150–151, 166
   reporting system for, 155–156
   scheduling of, 147–149
   specialists for, *see* specialists
   supervisors for, *see* supervisors
   union involvement in, 43–45,
      72, 150–151, 154, 171
   middle-down strategy, 72–76
   use of, in forming target group,
      133–134
minutes, meeting, as element of
   circle report, 155–156
misuse of quality circle
   avoiding, 188–189
   as resulting in disbanding circle,
      166–168
   see also control(s)

money, as incentive for quality
   circle participation, 20–21,
      25, 109, 111–112
monthly report, as element of circle report, 156
morale, quality circles as increasing, 11
moral principles, as organizational
   rules, 180–181, 184
motives, 109
   see also incentives

newsletters, use of, for recognition, 110

objectives, quality circle, 18,
   24–27
   designing, 65–66
   evaluation of, *see* evaluation
   informing organization of,
      47–49, 99
office, quality circle
   location of, determining, 56–58
   organizing, 58–64
   relationship of, to steering
      committee, 54
   role of, 41, 55
   top-down strategy and, 66
one-problem solution, as quality
   circle misconception, 48
organization
   attitude towards, 116
   authority within, 67, 74, 79, 82
   career advancement within, 25,
      112
   change within, 56, 107, 177–
      189
   decision making within, *see* deci-
      sion making
   division of labor within, 183
   effects of quality circle on,
      11–16, 177–189
   informing of quality circle
      start-up, to, 47–49, 99
   inter-, circle, 144–147
   management of, *see* manage-
      ment
   outcomes of, 125, 126–130
   as political system, 177–180
   power within, 180–182

preparing of, for quality circle program, 109–131
rules of, 180–181
outputs, circle, as mesurable data, 124–125
outside recognition, 111
overstaffing, quality circle, 60
ownership
  absence of, 79–80
  advisor as affecting, 86–95, 99, 116–119
  establishing, 52–53
  importance of, 66
  manager's, increasing, 76
  meeting schedule as affecting, 149
  spreading, 121, 133–136

Pareto analysis, as area of special training, 4, 23, 105
participation
  involuntary, 135–138
  limited, as misconception, 48
  as moral principle, 181
  motives for, 109–116
  recruiting for, *see* recruiting
  Toyota Auto Body's incentives for, 19, 20–21, 25
participative management, 99, 105
part-time advisors, 84, 91–95
  as consultants, 96–99
  see also advisors
personal outcomes, as measurable data, 125, 130–131
personnel, control over, 181–182
personnel records, as unavailable information, 152
pilot program, 72–78
pitfalls, quality circle
  absence of upper management approval as, 42–43, 51–52
  consultants and, 46–47
  disbanding circles and, 166–168
  during quality circle explanation, 47–51
  information restriction as, 151–155
  lack of central organizing unit as, 55–64

proposal implementation and, 119–123, 162–165
union involvement and, 43–45
political process, quality circle as, 177–189
power
  control of, 188–189
  limitations of, 184–188
  organizational, 180–182
  quality circle and, 182–184
preparation, importance of, in proposal presentations, 157
presentations
  as area of special training, 4, 102
  as growth evaluation tool, 165–166
  of proposals, 156–165
  see also implementation, proposal
principles, moral, as organizational rules, 180–181, 184
problem(s), *see* pitfalls, quality circle
problem-defined circle, 144
problem identification, as quality circle process, 14, 17, 105
problem solving
  as area of special training, 4, 23, 80, 104–105
  in integrated circles, 144
  one time, as quality circle misconception, 48
  quality circle as tool for, 11
  in task force circles, 138
  see also decision making
procedures, organizational, 180–181
process, quality circle, 14–17, 49
  see also quality circle
productivity
  as moral principle, 181
  quality circle as increasing, 11, 116
product quality
  as moral principle, 181
  quality circle as increasing, 11
professional association circle, as variation of quality circle, 138–141
profit sharing, as incentive, 112

program administrator
   as quality circle position, 58,
      59–61
   relationship of advisor to,
      85–95, 99
projects, quality circle, selection
   of, 4, 150–151, 166
promotion, quality circle, 21–23,
   26
   see also installation, quality circle
proposals, presentation of, 156–
   166
   see also presentations
proprietary information, as unavailable source, 152
punishment, as resulting from
   jural rule violation, 181

quality, product
   as moral principle, 181
   quality circle as increasing, 11,
      116
quality circle
   abuse of, avoiding, 188–189
   administrator for, 58–61
   advisors for, *see* advisors
   approval for, 41–43, 51–52
   change as resulting from, 56,
      107, 177–189
   codifying rules of, 168–171
   consultants for, 46–47, 53
   controls for, *see* control(s)
   decision making within, 4,
      179–180, 182–184
   defined, 3–4
   disbanding, 166–168
   effects of, 11, 16, 177–189
   employees' roles in, *see* employ-
      ees
   evaluation of, *see* evaluation
   explanation of, 47–51
   groups within, *see* group(s)
   growth of, 165–166
   inactivity of, 168
   incentives for, 20–21, 25–26,
      109–116
   installing, *see* installation, qual-
      ity circle
   integrated, 141–144
   interorganizational, 144–147

Japanese, 18–27
leader, *see* leader, quality circle
leading, 149–150
location of, 56–58
management's role in, *see* management
meetings for, *see* meetings, quality circle
misconceptions of, 48
objective of, 18, 24–27, 47–49,
   65–66, 99
office, 41, 54–64, 66
organization's role in, *see* organization
outputs, 124–125
overstaffing of, 60
ownership of, *see* ownership
participation in, *see* participation
as political process, 177–178
power within, 182–184
presentations by, 156–165
problems, *see* pitfalls, quality
   circle
problem solving within, 11, 138,
   144
process of, 14–17, 49
professional association, 138–
   141
progress of, 155–165, 173–174
projects for, 4, 150–151, 166
proposals, *see* implementation,
   proposal
recruiting members for, 134–
   135
report for, 155–156
selection of, 132–133
specialists for, *see* specialists
sponsorship of, 52–55
structure of, 14–17, 135–147
supervisor's role in, *see* supervisors
target, *see* target group
task force, 135–138
timetables for, 173–174
trainer's role in, *see* trainer
training, *see* training
union involvement in, 43–45,
   72, 150–151, 154, 171
variation within, 135–138

questionnaire, attitude
  as method of evaluation, 26
  use of, by advisor, 85

recognition, as motivating factor,
  109, 110–111
records, personnel, as unavailable
  information, 152
recruiting, 134–135
  task force circles and, 135–138
  see also participation
reform, political, 179–180
rehearsals, importance of, in proposal presentations, 157–158
relations, power, 177–189
report(s), progress, 155–156, 171
  as means of follow-up, 163
reporting, dual, 155–156
resistance to quality circle
  installation strategy to avoid,
    72–73
  as pitfall, 32, 58
resources, limiting of, as control
  method, 181–182
results
  measuring of, 123–131
  see also evaluation
review
  as quality circle process, 14, 17
  role of steering committee in,
    54
  see also evaluation
rewards, *see* incentives
roles
  teaching of, 102
  training as aiding, 101–102
  use of, in organizations, 180–
    182
rules
  codifying, 168–171
  as prescribed behavior, 180
  teaching of, 102, 105
  types of, 180–181

salary
  increasing, as participation in-
    centive, 20–21, 25, 109,
    111–112
  see also incentives
scheduling of meetings, 147–149

self-actualization, as motivating
  factor, 109
simultaneous training, 103
size, quality circle, 3
specialists
  importance of, 116–119
  role of, in quality circles, 4, 16,
    151–155
  Toyota Auto Body's use of, 20,
    25
  training of, *see* training
  see also advisors; consultants
sponsorship of quality circle program, 52–55
start-up program, *see* target group
steering committee, role of, 52
structure, quality circle, 14–17,
  135–147
study groups, 108
subgroups, functioning of, in organizations, 177–178
success, measuring of, 164
  see also evaluation
suggestion system, as incentive,
  111–112, 115–116
summary, as element of circle report, 155–156
supervisors
  absence of, as quality circle
    problem, 33–37, 73
  excluding, from quality circles,
    73, 78–84
  power relations of, 177–189
  program installation as respon-
    sibility of, 55
  relationship of advisors to, *see*
    advisors
  resistance of, 32, 56
  role of, 3, 15–17, 24, 183
  support, quality circle, 41
    importance of, 116–119
  use of steering committee for,
    52–55
  see also approval, quality circle
survey, attitude, 26, 85, 131

tardiness, quality circle as reducing, 11
target group
  approaching, 133–135

target group (*continued*)
  disbanding, 166–168
  growth of, evaluating, 165–166
  information sources for, 151–
    155
  leading, 149–150
  problems and projects for,
    150–151
  reporting progress of, 155–165
  rules for, 168–171
  scheduling meetings for, 147–
    149
  selection of, 132–133
  structure of, 14–17, 135–147
  timetables for, 173, 174
  see also installation, quality cir-
    cle; quality circle
task force circle, as variation of
  quality circle, 135–138
Taylor, Frederick W., on division
  of labor, 183
teaching, *see* training
teamwork, quality circle as increasing, 11, 116
technical facts, as organizational
  rules, 180–181
technical specialists, *see* specialists
timetable for program installation, 110, 173–174
tools, training, 102
  purchasing of, 103
top-down strategy, 66–72
  middle-down strategy and,
    72–84
Toyota Auto Body, 19–26, 51
trainer
  full-time advisor as, 85–91
  need for, 107

part-time advisor for, 91–95
as quality circle position, 58, 60
supervisor as, 80
training
  by advisors, *see* advisors
  of advisors, 106–107
  areas of, 4, 102–103
  of manager and technical
    specialists, 106
  as measure to avoid failure, 41
  of members, 104–105
  middle-down installation
    strategy as utilizing, 72–84
  need for, 100–102, 107
  objectives of, 104
  of part-time advisors, 93
  poor, as pitfall, 32
  simultaneous, 103

unions
  involvement of, in quality cir-
    cles, 43–45, 72, 171
  quality circles as avoidance of,
    150–151
  use of, as information source,
    154

variation, quality circle, 135–147
videotapes
  as reference tools, 48
  as training tool, 102
viewgraphs, as training tool, 102
voluntary participation, 4, 134–
  135
volunteers, part-time advisors as,
  91
volunteer steering committee, 54